fans

fans

JAMES MACKAY

CHARTWELL
BOOKS, INC.

This edition published in 2000 by
CHARTWELL BOOKS, INC.
A division of BOOK SALES, INC
114 Northfield Avenue,
Edison, New Jersey 08837

Produced by
PRC Publishing Ltd,
Kiln House, 210 New Kings Road, London SW6 4NZ

© 2000 PRC Publishing Ltd.

ISBN 0 78581 217 2

Printed and bound in China

Glossary

Appliqué	Any form of ornament added to the surface of sticks or guards, generally gold, silver, or gilt-brass pieces cast or stamped and set into the surface or attached by very fine pins.
Battoir	A type of fan with fewer than eight sticks, very wide at the top.
Brisé	A type of fan composed entirely of sticks joined together by ribbons.
Cartouche	A circular or oval frame containing a portrait or scene.
Chicken-skin	The skin of chickens was originally used to produce vellum or parchment of the very finest quality, a preferred medium for fan leaves. Later, the skins of animal foetuses were also used for this purpose.
Cockade	A type of folding fan which extends to a full circle.
Guards	The outer sticks of a fan, invariably larger and of more robust construction than the inner sticks or blades. Usually highly ornamented to form a decorative feature when the fan is closed.
Mount	An alternative term for leaf.
Piqué	Ornament composed of tiny gold or silver pins whose heads are flush with the surface of guards and sticks.
Reserve	That part of the fan leaf or blades containing the principal pictorial decoration.
Recto	Front.
Rivet	The pin which secures the foot of the sticks and guards, and often the subject of lavish ornament or attached to a tassle or loop.
Shoulder	The portion of the stick immediately below the leaf.
Spangles	Tiny, thin metal discs which came into fashion in the late 18th century and which were soon applied to dress accessories, especially fans. They were employed to enhance the decoration of fans as well as to reflect light from chandeliers.
Sticks	The pieces of wood, ivory, bone, or mother-of-pearl which form the framework of the fan.
Verso	Back.

Page 2: Marlene Dietrich, (see page 125).

CONTENTS

the *beginnings* of fans

1

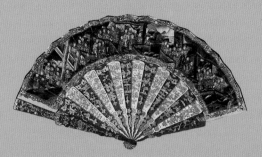

Fans are probably as old as mankind itself; it must have been almost instinctive for the first primitive man to grab hold of a palm-leaf, or even a bird's wing, and wave it rapidly in front of his face to provide a cooling breeze on the hottest day or to ward off insects. Such makeshifts scarcely deserve the designation of implement or tool, but they were just as useful and indispensable as the stone axe, the digging stick, or the wheel itself. For thousands of years such rudimentary fans were purely utilitarian, devoid of ornament and not of sufficient interest or importance to merit depiction in cave paintings. Out of these primitive objects would develop the fly-whisk or swatter, together with a multitude of fans in different shapes and sizes as well as countless materials and art forms.

The earliest type of fan of which we have record dates back more than five millennia, and was used in Egypt about 3200 BC. It is a long-handled pole fan symbolizing a person of very high rank and examples appear as part of the ornamental detail on a mace head of the Scorpion King from Hierakonopolis in Upper Egypt, late pre-Dynastic period, and now preserved in the Ashmolean Museum, Oxford. Clearly the fan had attained ceremonial importance by that date, and probably centuries earlier. Other examples of fans as symbols denoting importance and power have been recorded on stone carvings from tombs in Sumeria. A sarcophagus from Sakkarah, dated around 2300 BC, features a small hand fan; interestingly, it illustrates one of the other uses to which fans have been traditionally put—to beat the embers of a dying fire back to life. Any small flat object will do just as well, as any boy scout will tell you, but out of the simple fire fans there gradually developed the bellows.

Right: Plumed royal pole-fans in pharaonic Egypt: Moses is found amongst the reeds on the river bank by the Pharaoh's daughter and her entourage, from the 19th century engraving by Gustave Doré.

Previous page: The Queen of Sheba (see page 57).

Left: Pole fans as a badge of royalty seem to have developed globally at an early period. This engraving by Nicholas de Challeaux (January 1565) shows a native American queen being transported to the home of her new husband, escorted by a retinue which includes two fan-bearers.

Right: An Egyptian wall fresco in the tomb of the Vizier Rekhmire at Thebes depicting a banqueting scene, in which pole fans are much in evidence.

Examples of actual fans from pharaonic Egypt date from 1657 BC. The earliest now extant, preserved in the museum at Boulac, consists of a pole with a flat wooden paddle at one end. Across the top of the paddle is a series of holes into which would have been inserted ostrich feathers. In the tomb of the Tutankhamun (1350 BC) Howard Carter discovered several fans, including the boy-pharaoh's personal fan made of gold, with repoussé decoration showing him hunting ostriches to provide the very plumes of this fan. The reverse shows the hunting party returning with a brace of ostriches, Tutankhamun proudly carrying the feathers under his arm. Elsewhere in the shrine Carter came upon the fans of two royal princes, one wrought in sheet gold and the other of ebony overlaid with gold and encrusted with semi-precious stones. More than 3,500 years after the interment Carter noted that sufficient vestiges of the plumes remained for him to determine that they were alternately white and brown, 42 feathers to each fan.

The peculiar circumstances of pharaonic burial practices have ensured that we know more about the fans of Egypt 4,000 years ago than we do of any other part of the world. Some scholars have theorized about the spread of fans from Egypt to Babylon, Indiaz, and the Near East, and to Greece and Rome, but while Egyptian influence on the fans of the Alexandrine empire, and thence Rome, is obvious, it is more likely that ceremonial fans developed quite independently in India and Ceylon (Sri Lanka). From documentary evidence as well as folklore it seems certain that fans of one sort or another were in existence in China even earlier

than in Egypt although surviving examples do not predate the fans from the tomb of Tutankhamun.

The Greek historian Euripides mentions the fan as an import from "barbarous" (i.e. non-Greek speaking) lands, and certainly there is ample pictorial evidence for this, notably in friezes and the decoration of bowls and vases which show Greek fans in considerable detail, both small, hand-held fans and large pole fans festooned with feathers set in ornamental wooden handles. Greek fans of the classical period might take the form of a pair of broad wings joined laterally to a long handle, or a cluster of feathers radiating from a circular mount. In early fans the feathers waved freely, but by the fourth century BC they were often kept more rigid by threads connecting them near the base as well as across the top.

The Romans greatly extended the use of fans, diversifying the range of shapes and sizes. Both Apuleius and Virgil describe the Eleusinian mysteries and Bacchic festivals in which ornate fans were borne in ceremonial procession. A small fan one could handle oneself, but a large fan required the services of a slave or attendant, and thus it came to symbolize gentility and aristocracy, just as it had denoted princely or regal rank in Egypt. Ornate fans would later play a prominent role in the ritual of the Greek Orthodox and Coptic Christian faiths and through the Byzantine Empire would be re-imported into Italy as an element in Catholic ceremony as well.

To the large screen fans for providing a cooling breeze, and the small rigid fans that coaxed a fire into life, may be added a third type, of much more robust construction and a large, flat wooden spade shape. This was used to shovel up loose grain and toss it into the air to separate the wheat from the chaff. Such a fan was called a "winnow"—and this brings us to the extraordinary family of words, found in many languages, meaning many different things but all closely related. The English word winnow now means to weed out, sort out, or separate, and it is easy to see how these metaphorical usages have come from the original notion of separating grain from chaff by exposing it to a current of air. The word may be traced back to Middle English winnewen and Old English windwian, Old High German

winton and thence to the Latin vannus from which we also derive the word vane. There is also van, in the original meaning of a winnowing device, a word still used in the north of England, and, of course, fan itself, via Old English fann. The Latin word vannus was restricted to one kind of fan, that used for winnowing grain, and, in turn, it was derived from ventus, wind. Along this particular route the Romance languages got their words for a fan: éventail (French), ventaglio (Italian) and abanillo (Spanish). Similarly the German word Wanne is restricted to a winnowing-fan, and later came to signify a tub, pail, or bath. To denote a fan in the sense of a personal cooling device the Germans prefer the word Fächer which comes from Fach, a division, compartment, cell, or panel.

When it came to fans for other uses, the Romans had separate words. Flabellum (from flabrum, a blast of wind) meant a device for creating a little wind. Then there was ventilabrum (from ventus, wind and labrum, edge or lip) from which came the verb ventilare, to fan, which could also mean to excite or provoke. While flabellum seems to have been confined to small cooling fans, ventilabrum denoted large pole fans, for cooling as well as for winnowing corn. Both terms were taken over by the medieval church and came to apply to large fans used in ecclesiastical ritual. The Romans also had the muscarium (from musca, a fly) which, though often applied indiscriminately to fans, was originally confined to those fans which doubled as fly-whisks. Just as fly-whisks are used in some African countries to this day as a badge of rank, so also the small fan would, over the centuries, become an indispensable costume accessory for both sexes at various times and in different parts of the world.

Although the Chinese had large screen fans to ventilate rooms and pole fans wielded by slaves, they are indelibly associated with the development of the small fan, intended for individual use. According to legend, the personal fan was invented by a girl at the Feast of Lanterns when everyone wore a mask. Stifled by her mask in the searing heat of the day, the girl ripped it off and used it to fan herself. The other ladies present were not slow to follow her example. Whether there is any truth in this hoary old

legend (did masks antedate fans?) is immaterial; what matters is that hand-held fans obviously went back a very long way. Apart from this unknown maiden, the invention of the fan has been credited to various emperors: Hsein Yuan (2699 BC), Shun (2255 BC), or Wee-wang (1122 or 1106 BC). The last named is too late, for there is also the story of the emperor Kao-tsong (1323–1266 BC) who would only have fans consisting of the feathers of the pheasant which he regarded as a particularly lucky bird. Not surprisingly, the feathers of the peacock were also very much in demand for this purpose, while other feathers were often dyed in bright colors. Thereafter references to fans in ancient Chinese literature become more frequent, and it is obvious that they were well-established before the end of the second millennium BC.

The art of constructing feather fans has been practiced in China for thousands of years. Not only were the feathers carefully chosen for the symmetry of their patterns and the graduated tones of color, but even more elaborate fans were composed of the feathers of different species, often overlapping to provide contrasting bands of color. Despite literary references of great antiquity, pictorial representations are of relatively recent vintage, around the beginning of the Christian era and confined to statuary, bas-reliefs, and friezes from the Han dynasty. Sufficient images have survived to confirm that, by that time, a very wide range of fans was in existence: circular, oval, palmate, heart-shaped, or even irregular, slightly pear-shaped being cited. From the intricate details of the carving it appears that fans were plaited from grasses or fine slivers of young bamboo as well as palm-leaves reinforced by a bamboo spine. Both pictorial and documentary evidence reveals that bamboo fans were elaborately painted, while others were ingeniously wrought from tortoiseshell plates riveted together, or panels of silk, chicken-skin, or paper mounted in bamboo frames fitted to carved wooden or ivory handles.

The small circular or rounded square fans with leaves of silk, parchment, or paper positively encouraged painted ornament. According to the chronicles, the noted scholar Wang Hsi-chih (AD 321–79) came across an old woman hawking plain paper fans. On impulse he seized them and hurriedly wrote a few inscriptions on them. The pedlar was furious at this act of vandalism on her nice, clean fans, but she was mollified when they sold like hot cakes. As a result, Wang came to be known as the "Sage of Calligraphy," and established the long-standing tradition of writing as an art form, often seen to good advantage on Chinese fan leaves. There is also the story of Princess Pan, about AD 550, a concubine of Chi'eng Si. When she was thrown over for a younger lady, Pan sent the emperor a paper fan on which she wrote a rather pathetic poem, likening herself to a fan which is indispensable in the height of summer but is discarded when autumn comes. From this story came the Chinese expression "autumn fan" to describe a deserted wife.

The type employed by Princess Pan would eventually develop into the album fan, made of lightly colored paper but otherwise quite plain, which was used as a medium for sending the Chinese equivalent of Valentine's Day cards, leaving the calligraphy and ornament to the individual lover.

All of the early fans had one thing in common: they had a fixed or rigid leaf. While fans of this type have continued right down to the present day, the folding fan was a relative newcomer, supposedly devised in Japan around AD 670. The story goes that the anonymous artist got the idea from the structure of a bat's wings, the opportunity to study them arising when one of these creatures got trapped in his bedroom, flew into a lamp in its panic, and burned its wings so badly that it crashed to the floor. As this incident took place in the short reign of Jen-Ji (668–72), the invention of the *Hiro ogi* (literally "wide end fan") can be dated fairly precisely. Folding fans spread to China a century later when one of them was offered as a tribute to the emperor by "the barbarians of the south-east" who were mocked and ridiculed as a result. This anecdote may well explain why folding fans (known as *Tsin theou chen*) were so slow to win acceptance in China. According to tradition, they did not make much headway in China until the advent of the Ming dynasty in the second half of the 14th century, and never completely ousted the rigid fan. Actual examples of early Chinese fans are surprisingly rare, the oldest extant specimens being a pair of woven bamboo fans dating from the second century BC; they were discovered in the Mawangdui tomb near Changsha (Hunan). Even survivors from later periods, down to the 16th century, are very elusive in view of the fragile nature of their components, and the majority are confined to museum collections. Only fragments of fans from Greece and Rome now exist. During the Dark Ages the fan, like so many other refinements of Roman civilization, vanished from the scene, only to be gradually revived as the barbaric races that overwhelmed the Roman Empire themselves acquired a veneer of civilization. In the early medieval period the Roman *flabellum* was revived as a silver or gilt disc mounted on a long handle, carried by deacons to ward the flies off the sacramental vessels; but apart from references to such articles in church inventories, no examples of this type of fan are now extant.

Right: A circular, rigid pole fan designed for the use of a Chinese emperor, now on display in the Forbidden City, Beijing.

Apart from two plaited straw fans dating from the early sixth century, recovered from a tomb at Akhmin and believed to be of Saracenic origin, the earliest European fan now in existence is the celebrated fan which belonged to Queen Theodolinda of Lombardy who died in 628. Dating around the end of the sixth century, it is remarkable not only for its revolutionary design but also its beautiful condition, preserved as it was in the shrine of the queen who brought Christianity to the Lombards. Here, in the basilica of St. John the Baptist which she built at Monza, Theodolinda's fan, one of her most prized possessions, was kept in its original wooden case, complete with its contemporary silver mount and inscribed in Latin verse using the Lombardic script.

What is particularly remarkable about this fan is its construction, for it is made of pleated purple vellum, the folds compressing, concertina fashion, into the case, or opening out like a cockade to form an almost complete circle. Because of its startling appearance, doubts have sometimes been cast on its provenance, although there is a somewhat similar cockade fan, the famous *Tournus Flabellum*, which dates from the 11th century and is now preserved in the National Museum, Florence. Theodolinda's fan was regarded as a sacred relic, which girls touched for good luck on the eve of their marriage, but its existence outside Monza was apparently unknown until 1857 when the English architect William Burges visited the basilica and subsequently published an illustrated account of it in the *Archaeological Journal*.

It would be almost a thousand years after Theodolinda before fans reappeared in Europe in any appreciable quantity. In the intervening period it would be left to the countries of the Far East to maintain an unbroken tradition and raise the fan to the status of an art form.

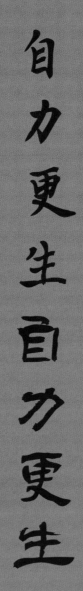

Asian fans

2

China, with its sophisticated technology in the manufacture of silks and other textiles as well as paper, had an enormous head-start over the rest of the world in the manufacture of fans, but from the collector's standpoint it is the fans from the 17th and later centuries which pass through the sale-room regularly. By the middle of the 16th century, when China was beginning to open up to trade with the Portuguese and later the Dutch, there were many different kinds of fan in regular production. Small rigid fans of various materials, mostly with painted decoration, were still very fashionable, although they were now overtaken by folding fans.

What had once been derided as a barbarian invention, the folding fan went through a long period during which it was regarded as the badge of the courtesan (the prostitutes of the seaports allegedly picking up the notion from Japanese seamen), but eventually its usefulness overcame the barriers of decency and became fashionable with respectable ladies as well.

As the folding fan became more socially acceptable, so the styles and materials used widened enormously. The basic form consisted of more or less semicircular pieces of paper or silk mounted on a number of thin sticks of bamboo or sandalwood riveted together at the foot. When folded, the fan was protected by guard sticks, usually of ivory. The sticks themselves were generally quite plain and unadorned, such ornament as there was being confined to the guard sticks in which the techniques of filigree ornament became highly developed.

Instead, the skills of the painter and calligrapher were lavished on the fan leaves. The fact that the leaves were regarded more highly than the fans

Right: A pair of Manchu ladies, dating around the end of the 19th century. The lady on the right is carrying a small rigid fan of lantern shape.

Previous page: Canton fan of 1820 (see page 21).

Left: A group of Chinese men and boys, dating from the 1890s, showing that folding fans were an indispensable fashion accessory carried by both sexes, regardless of age.

Right: A Canton gilt-metal filigree fan of about 1820, enameled in blue, green and purple with a motif of scrolling flowers.

as such is reflected in the Chinese passion for removing the leaves from their sticks and mounting them in albums and guardbooks. Fan leaves, in effect, became scroll paintings in miniature. Fans with impressionistic motifs painted by a few deft brush-strokes and often accompanied by inscriptions were regularly exchanged in court circles, much as we might exchange picture postcards with friends and relatives. There was something almost, but not quite, ephemeral about these paper fans, for their leaves would invariably be treasured for posterity, even if the sticks were very soon discarded.

Fan painters, accepting the challenge of this restrictive medium, raised minimalism to a high art; space and perspective were often conveyed by little more than two or three brush strokes against a blank ground. The painted fan, in essence, represented the very acme of the minuscule arts in China and later also in Japan and Korea where Chinese styles were slavishly copied for centuries. Although the various conventions in Chinese painting had been established thousands of years ago, any tendency towards monotony or stereotyping was countered by the development of count-

less regional and local styles. By the time of the Ming dynasty it would probably be true to say that every city, town, and country district had evolved its own distinctive methods of painting, types of color and forms of ornamentation, not to mention regional variations in the actual construction and composition of the fans themselves. In addition, different styles were developed to suit the tastes of every class of society from the lowliest peasant to the highest rank of mandarin and from court ladies to courtesans.

Often the materials used reflected their availability in different parts of China. At one extreme, for example, were the highly distinctive jade-plaque rigid fans of Chekiang, utilizing a particularly large species of bamboo that grew in that province, from which were cut large pieces, generally flat with a slight curve. From Hangchow came the oiled fan, so-called from the black oiled paper derived from the bark of the persimmon, with up to 50 sticks. Incidentally, black and other very dark colors were originally associated with the peasantry, but during the 19th century there was a radical change in outlook, with the result that black, especially inlaid with gold, became

21

Above: A mid-19th century fan from Canton, both sides lacquered in black and gold, showing figures promenading on terraces. The ornamentation of this fan also incorporates an array of Taoist symbols.

Above: A fine Canton fan of about 1860,
the leaf painted with figures on terraces,
and the ivory sticks carved with figures
and alternately stained red.

acceptable, indeed highly desirable, to even the highest classes of society. Both Canton and Beijing were noted centers for the production of fans with hidden scenes. When the fan was opened in the normal manner, from left to right, a perfectly respectable picture emerged; but when the fan was opened from right to left a highly erotic image emerged instead.

The painstaking technique of lacquer was also applied to fans from a relatively early period, though later refinements included the addition of different colours as well as gold dust. Chinese lacquered fans remained essentially two-dimensional and it was left to the Japanese to take this technique forward by combining successive layers with skillful cutting to achieve quite startling three-dimensional effects.

Ivory fans came into fashion in China about the 15th century and thereafter grew in importance, especially after the establishment of an ivory factory within the precincts of the imperial palace at Beijing in the 17th century. At first fretting, piercing, and carving were applied to the sticks, which were still covered by paper or silk fan leaves, but subsequently the Chinese developed the brisé fan in which paper was dispensed with and the fan itself consisted entirely of broad, flat sticks which were intricately carved. Mother-of-pearl, tortoiseshell, and sandalwood were treated in a similar fashion to create some of the most beautiful brisé fans of the 18th and early 19th centuries. In many cases the decorative effect was achieved solely by carving and fretting the material itself, but in others these techniques were combined with filigree inlays and enamel painting. The so-called mandarin fan had sticks of carved and decorated ivory, combined with a silk or paper fanleaf on which the faces of people were minutely carved and painted in ivory and even their costumes consisted of tiny pieces of silk.

In his *History of the Fan* (1910), George W. Rhead states that in Japan the fan was regarded as an emblem of life itself, symbolized by the sticks widening and expanding from the rivet. From this the fan came to be very closely bound up with every aspect of the life, work and customs of the Japanese. Fans were exchanged as New Year gifts and

Left: Two Japanese ladies, photographed in 1915, preparing for the ritual of the tea ceremony. Both are clad in kimonos and carry small painted hand-screen fans.

on all manner of special occasions. Fans were carried by both sexes in every walk of life; even the condemned man mounted the scaffold, fan in hand. Special fans with iron handles were developed for the samurai and, decorated with heraldic symbols, were used in battle for signaling the deployment of troops. The earliest type, known as *Gumpai Uchiwa*, had flat iron leaves but by the 12th century the *Gun Sen* or iron folding fan, had been developed for the same purpose, fitted with leaves of stout paper and painted in red and gold on a black or dark-colored background.

Not only did the Japanese invent the folding fan, but they also developed it to a higher degree than the Chinese. The earliest type had 15 bamboo sticks but gradually the number of sticks increased until the court fans of the 11th century boasted up to 38 sticks. Early fans had an arc of little more than 90 degrees when fully extended, but eventually fans opened to

Above: Japanese actors performing with fans in a Kagura Noh play. As an art form, Noh is a dance drama heavily influenced by the principles of Zen Buddhism and only employs male actors. Note the asymmetrical ornament of the fan leaves and the decorative streamers attached to the edges.

Left: A fine Japanese brisé fan, dating around 1880, lacquered with the seven stages of the bamboo grove. The ivory leaves have been delicately worked in pen and ink with gold inlay.

180 degrees or even beyond. The elaborate court fans, known as *Akome Ogi* and developed in the 11th century, had elaborate rivets in the form of a bird or butterfly, were often extravagantly decorated at the corners with silk or paper flowers, and had foot-long streamers attached to the handles. This type remained fashionable up until the Meiji Revolution in 1868.

The *Mai Ogi* or dancing fan developed early in the 17th century. As its name suggests, it was extensively used by dancers and jugglers and was therefore simple and robust in construction, generally with 10 or 12 sticks and a leaf of thick paper decorated with some sort of armorial device. The *Rikin Ogi* or tea fan was invented about the same time and was used thereafter in connection with the elaborate tea ceremony. It was unusual in its design, having no more than three sticks and a simple leaf with the minimum of decoration. Its chief purpose was to serve as a tray for handing round the small cakes and it would have been a grave breach of etiquette to use it to fan oneself. Even more utilitarian were the water fans, intended solely for use in the kitchen and developed in the 18th century.

Like their Chinese counterparts, Japanese fans gave expression to the greatest artistry, but developed a much greater range of styles and treatments. Unlike the minimalist treatment found in Chinese fan leaves, the Japanese believed in lavish illustrations and exuberant colors, often enriched with gold leaf. Until the middle of the 18th century the pictures on Japanese fans have a flat, two-dimensional appearance but when Occidental notions of light and shade and, above all, perspective began to influence large-scale paintings, these concepts were rapidly taken up by fan painters as well. Another aspect of folding fans which was characteristically Japanese was the use of block printing, which reached its zenith in the late 18th and early 19th centuries, under the influence of Harunobo, Hiroshige, and Hokusai. Fans of this period are replete with genre scenes from everyday life, in the style of the Ukiyoe (pictures of the fleeting world) which were then very fashionable.

What gives the fans of China and Japan an added dimension was the fact that so many of them, from the late 17th century onward, were

Right: A group of six Oriental fans, mid to late 19th century, including a very fine Japanese fan with a genre landscape on the silk leaf (lower left), a mandarin fan richly decorated in red and blue (lower right), and a black lacquered fan with ornament in mother-of-pearl and silver filigree (upper right).

Far right: The two lower fans in this group are respectively a very rare topographical fan from Hong Kong, not long after it was ceded to Britain in 1841, and a beautiful mandarin fan from Canton, dating around the end of the 18th century. The upper fans are English, mid-19th century.

exported to Europe. Within the ensuing century, moreover, fans were being produced and decorated in China specifically for this export market, just as porcelain was produced for the same purpose. Similarly, while the vast majority of fans were virtually mass-produced with rather stereotyped motifs, and then distributed through wholesale and retail outlets in various parts of Europe, there was increasingly a lucrative business in the production of fans (like porcelain) to specific order, hence the examples from about 1780 onwards which may be found with the owner's monogram or heraldic crest. The Chinese were adept at giving westerners what they wanted: either Chinese motifs suitably modified to suit western taste, or western motifs rendered in a distinctly Oriental manner. Either way, the end results were amusing, thought-provoking and utterly charming.

Apart from their subject matter, however, Chinese export fans often differed quite radically from the fans intended for domestic consumption in the range of materials employed. Where indigenous fans were restrained, export fans were florid and exuberant, delighting in the use of mother-of-

pearl inlays, gold and silver filigree work, enameling, lacquer and japanning. The parallel with export porcelain is reflected in the fact that fans were often painted with the same motifs, perhaps exploiting images which had already proved popular with Europeans. As the 18th century wore on, export fans tended to become larger. Originally the ivory leaves that made up these fans were extensively painted, but later on the painted areas were reduced to small cartouches or omitted altogether, whereas the carving and fretting became correspondingly more important. A characteristic of late-18th century fans was a ribbed ground on which was worked floral ornament and vignettes of scenery and buildings. This style was taken a stage further in the early 19th century which witnessed the rise of ribbed ivory fans dominated by much greater attention to the ornamentation of the guard sticks than had previously been the case, together with genre scenes and figures. Towards the middle of the century, however, the quality of carving generally deteriorated, fans decreased in size and the sticks were noticably thicker.

Left: This group of European fans dating between 1750 and 1790 includes a Chinese gilt filigree fan of about 1830 (lower right).

Right: An excellent example (below) of a Japanese brisé fan dating around 1880, the finely carved ivory leaves depicting cranes in flight or alighting amid bamboo.

Right, middle: Japanese ivory brisé fan from about 1890, lacquered and decorated with gold of different shades in hiramakie and takamakie styles.

Right, below: A late-19th century Japanese brisé fan. The ivory leaves have been lacquered in gold of various shades and textures to create a spirited scene of figures in a landscape.

Below: Both Chinese and Japanese fans were often decorated with calligraphy (handwriting), applied to paper or silk painted leaves with a brush and ink.

Brisé fans with black and gold lacquer ornament were developed for the export market around the beginning of the 19th century. Early examples were comparatively small but gradually became bigger towards the middle of the century. These lacquer fans were noted for their scrolling foliage and floral decoration within which was often placed a shield bearing the owner's arms or cypher. In parallel with the design developments of the ivory fans, lacquer fans of the 1820s and 1830s began appearing with figural and scenic motifs. By mid-century lacquer fans were quite large and their sticks much thinner, with lavish decoration on both sides. A startling innovation of this period was the introduction of a polychrome panel.

A very wide range of subjects was depicted on the fans produced in the second half of the 19th century. The most popular motifs were those which featured aspects of everyday life in China, ranging from simple pastoral scenes to elaborate court pageantry. Fans were often issued in thematic sets with a range of related subjects, such as agricultural scenes or different trades and occupations. Others concentrated on the fauna and flora of China, fans depicting flowers, birds, and insects being especially popular. There were also useful fans which reproduced street maps. It was during this period that the mandarin fan attained its zenith, as craftsmen vied with each other in producing fans with more and more figures, their painted ivory faces and intricate costumes filling every part of the leaf.

Japanese fans were little known outside their own country until the mid-19th century when, following Commodore Peary's expedition of 1853, Japan began to open up to trade with the west. This accelerated considerably from 1868, after the overthrow of the Shogunate and the resumption of active political power by the Emperor Meiji who embarked on a ruthless policy of westernization. Ironically, as the Japanese hastened to embrace the technology, customs, dress, and lifestyle of the west, their art and artifacts became widely known in Europe and America for the first time. From 1875 onwards the craze for all things Japanese affected fans

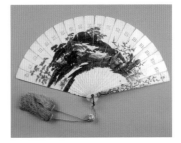

which were exported in astronomical numbers. It has been estimated that more than 15 million fans were exported in 1891 alone. Inevitably supply was hard-pressed to cope with such a demand and as a result the quality of execution, both of the fans themselves and their decoration, suffered. The demand for Japanese fans coincided with a curious style in interior decoration around the turn of the century which favored large screens and wall-hangings to which fans were affixed at random to create a japonais-erie effect. This craze was relatively short-lived, however, for the fan as a fashion accessory was in decline by the end of the 19th century and had

all but vanished from the scene before the outbreak of the First World War.

Ironically, western interest in oriental fans as collectables only began to developed at a time when fans in general went out of everyday use. An exhibit of Chinese fans at the Great Exhibition of 1851 in London excited some comment by Tallis, who wrote the official history of the exhibition. After extolling the superiority of Chinese fans over their European (mainly French) imitators, he noted that the chief centers of production for the export market were Canton Soochow, Hangchow,

Above: A colorful group of Japanese paper fans.

Above: Korean children performing a fan dance.

Right: A Chinese master fan maker at work, adding the intricate detail to a picture with a fine brush (often consisting of a single bristle).

Far right: A Chinese lady using her fan at the opera. Folding fans are still very much in everyday use in the Far East.

and Nankin, that those made of ivory and bone were produced exclusively for export, the Chinese themselves preferring the paper folding type. Significantly the displays at the exhibition had not come from China directly but were organized by three English firms of importers, Braine, Daniell and Hewett who wholesaled fans at from 10d (4p=6.5c) to 14s 6d ($1.18) a dozen. It makes one wonder what the Chinese craftsmen received by way of payment.

Although the fans of China and Japan dominated the imports from Asia in the 19th century they were not the only ones by any means. The

Dutch, Spanish, and British, through their colonial empires in the East Indies, the Philippines, and India, became aware of the fans produced in these areas and these were imported into Europe along with other distinctive wares. The more traditional fans of India and the Indies were rigid, often circular or heart-shaped, with a central spine of split ivory or wood, a split cane frame, and a covering of silk or linen, often intricately embroidered and enhanced by the judicious use of silver or gold metallic threads. Distinctive forms included a flag shape in which the

Above: Close-up of a Buddhist monk in Phnom-Penh carrying an umbrella and a large feather fan.

Above: Hakka women holding up their fans to shield their faces from the gaze of strangers.

richly embroidered fan was attached by one edge to a small pole; examples were produced in many parts of India as well as in Burma and Thailand.

Cockade fans with brisé leaves of ivory or hardwoods spiraling out to form a full circle from a central rivet were produced in Ceylon, the Indies, the Philippines, and other islands of the western Pacific and Indian oceans, fans with a double cockade being a speciality of the Seychelles using the exotic wood of the Coco-de-Mer palm. Brisé fans with broad, thin sandalwood sticks were very fashionable in the Indies and Malaysia, doubtless

Left: A small boy holding a rigid screen fan.

Right: A Miaos woman in ceremonial dress and jewelry, with folding fans in both hands.

Below right: A Balinese dancer with an open fan. Leather fans were particularly popular all over Indonesia, especially in dances. Such fans were brightly painted and richly gilded, often with motifs derived from the Wayang shadow puppets.

influenced by Chinese forms, although they took on distinctive local variations, such as the ornately carved handles of the Malay peninsula and the curvilinear sticks favored in Ceylon (Sri Lanka).

Folding fans with paper or silk leaves were also widely produced in Burma, Thailand, and the Indies in imitation of Chinese styles but recognizable on account of local subjects, especially scenery and figure groups which, of course, can be identified by their costume. Fans with floral or bird motifs were produced in the Philippines during the 19th century in emulation of Chinese export wares and were destined for the Spanish market.

Although Indian fans never attained anything approaching the importance of their Chinese counterparts, and therefore tended towards the more utilitarian and less decorative forms, nevertheless many different regional types, both in materials and construction, emerged over the centuries. Apart from ivory which was both cheap and plentiful, Indian fans were produced in a wide range of textile fabrics, notably in the Punjab which had an immense reputation for sumptuous embroidery. Indian taste demanded that such fans be extravagantly worked with metallic thread and spangles of gold or silver, on a ground of rich, deep color. At the other end of the spectrum, however, the Moslem districts of India, especially Hyderabad and Kashmir, as well as Persia and Afghanistan, made extensive use of papier-mâché and varnishes to produce numerous forms of rigid fans. A speciality of the Maldive Islands was a type of fan composed of layers of lacquer in contrasting colors which were intricately cut away to reveal different colors.

Left: A British official in India (1900) receives a pedicure from an Indian servant, while the punkawallah keeps his master cool with a large circular fan.

Right: A group of British officers relaxing in the Persian seaport of Bushire in January 1910. Note the curious mixture of European and Persian dress, the hookah pipe, and the outsize folding fan held by the gentleman on the extreme right.

Below right: A large folding fan shaped like a peacock, the sticks carved in a composite motif to form the body of the bird.

Below: A carnival party-goer in China wearing an elaborate costume and carrying a finely decorated fan.

Western *styles*

3

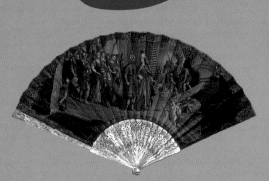

Apart from stray references, both pictorial and written, to *flabella* in the medieval Church, fans as such disappeared in Europe between the fall of the Roman Empire at the beginning of the fifth century and the closing years of the 13th century. Even in ecclesiastical ritual use of fans seems to have all but died out by the 11th century, remembered only by fragments such as jeweled mounts and handles preserved in museum collections, or in tantalizing details in church inventories. Various royal inventories in Italy and France from the 1280s onward carry fleeting references to ornamental fans. From the terminology employed, it appears that they were chiefly used as fly-whisks or swatters. French inventories describe them under the word *esmouchoir* (from the Latin *musca*, a fly), while an inventory of Isabella of France (1292–1358), wife of Edward II of England, refers in Latin to "two whips (*flagella*) for chasing flies." Bearing in mind that *flabella* were intended to ward flies and insects off chalices and sacramental dishes, the confusion of terms is understandable. By Tudor times various cockade or pleated fans were beginning to appear in portraits of royalty, including quite large types out of which would evolve a form of umbrella or parasol. Small rigid fans made of leather, often impregnated with perfume, were used in Spain by the end of the Middle Ages and may have resulted from Moorish influence. Small feather fans were also in use in the Mediterranean countries by the early 16th century, probably also developed as a result of contact with north Africa and the Near East. Their entry into France is well documented, for Catherine de Medici is recorded as possessing feather fans when she married Henri II of France in 1549, and that the fashion was rapidly taken up by the ladies of the royal court.

Right: Catherine of Valois (1401–37), daughter of King Charles VI of France, who became Queen of England through her marriage to King Henry V in 1420. In this engraving of about 1420 she is portrayed at Troyes, holding a very elaborately carved and turned, rigid fan of a type then used by royal ladies mainly as a fly-swatter.

Previous page: Early 18th century fan (see page 55).

Hans liefrinck

43

1

2

3

4

1 A French handscreen of about 1770 depicting Annette and Lubin in a scene from the opera of that name by Marmontel.

2 A French card handscreen of about 1770 painted with an urn of exotic flowers, the verso with a spray of blue flowers.

3 A French handscreen of about 1770. On one side appears a hand-colored etching of a lady and two gentlemen, while the other side reproduces a map of Italy by Robert de Vaugondy.

4 A French printed handscreen of about 1775, the mount painted with trophies of love on a pink background.

5   A shaped Italian handscreen covered in blue watered paper and applied with a colored aquatint of three archaeologists and two builders in a ruined abbey, signed by P. Oggioni.

6   A French handscreen in the Directoire style at the beginning of the 19th century, applied with an oval stipple engraving of a goddess.

7   A French shaped handscreen of about 1815, with an oval stipple engraving of "La Mère Adorée," framed with pressed gold paper.

8   A French hexagonal handscreen of mauve card applied with an oval hand-colored stipple engraving, circa 1819. The brown spotting is foxing caused by iron impurities in the paper. Although such blemishes detract from the appearance of fans, relative rarity makes them admissible.

5

6

7

8

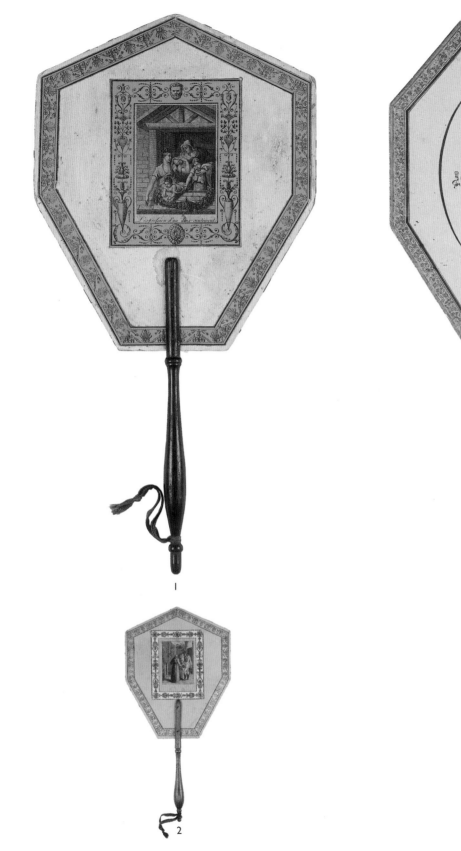

1

3

1,2 A pair of French heptagonal hand-screens dating about 1829. Matched pairs such as this are very desirable.

3,4 A pair of French octagonal hand-screens of about 1820, signed by Marie Deplasse and featuring an armillary sphere and map.

2

4

5 An octagonal handscreen of pink card of about 1820 applied with an engraving of a Swiss view showing a church with three figures and cattle in the foreground.

6 One of a pair of embroidered hand-screens of about 1870, the shaped blue-satin mounts painted with scenes of lovers on stepping stones.

7 A shaped handscreen of about 1840 covered in green watered paper applied with a chromolithograph of two little girls feeding a sheep.

8,9 An unusual pair of rectangular handscreens from the Netherlands in 1826, in the form of open books.

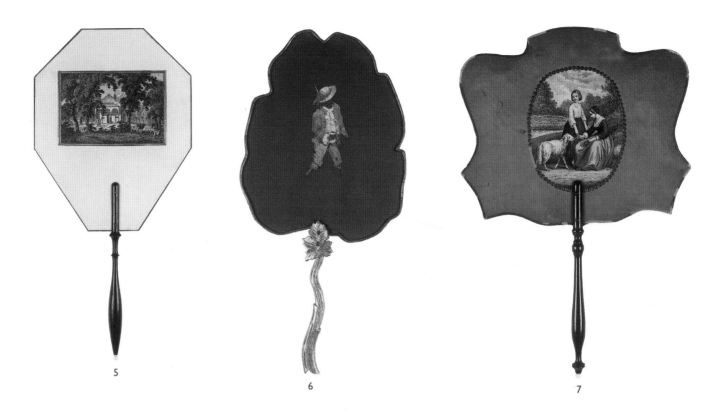

5

6

7

8

9

Left: A standing portrait of King James VI of Scotland and I of England, with his wife, Anne of Denmark, engraved by Renold Elstracke in 1605, two years after James succeeded to the English throne. The queen is shown holding a fan in her left hand.

Right: Portrait in oils (1616) of Matoaka, better known as Pocahontas (1595–1617), the daughter of the Native American chief Powhatan. Following her conversion to Christianity and marriage to settler John Rolfe she changed her name to Rebecca Rolfe. This painting, executed in the last year of her short life, shows her in the height of Jacobean fashion, but the feather fan she carries owes much to Native American influence.

Ætatis suæ 21. Aº. 1616.

Although rigid fans were largely superseded by folding fans, they did not disappear by any means and, in fact, there was a remarkable revival in the half century between 1770 and 1820, the heyday of the small handscreen as they are more generally known. They were usually made of stout card, although other materials, such as leather or hide, were used. The usual shape is a rounded, baroque shield or inverted pear, particularly in the early period; but toward the end of the 18th century various fancy shapes came into fashion and ranged from plain, scrolled or chamfered horizontal rectangles, ovals, and polygons to completely irregular forms. At the beginning of the 19th century the prevailing Directoire style in France demanded that handscreens be almost semi-circular with a curvilinear base. Sometimes two or more layers of card were superimposed, in contrasting background colors.

Handscreens were either entirely painted by hand or had stipple engraving or etching which could then be colored by hand. The handscreen had a definite advantage over the folding fan when it came to the depiction of a single, relatively large scene, for it did not suffer from the usual strictures of being curved and then subjected to folds and pleats. Consequently the vignettes on handscreens were usually much larger and more lavish in their decoration, and some very striking effects were achieved. Different motifs might appear on both recto (front) and verso (back), while handscreens produced as matched pairs are particularly desirable. They may be found with words and music or even detailed maps, complementing scenic vignettes. By the 1830s some handscreens were being produced with chromolithographed motifs, but by that time the fashion was on the wane, and it had virtually died out by the middle of the century. The chief drawback about the handscreen was its rigidity: it lacked the discreet convenience and versatility of the folded fan that would eventually entirely eclipse the handscreen.

It must be emphasized that such examples were relatively isolated and confined to the uppermost classes of society; they did not constitute any general usage of fans in Europe before the middle of the 16th century when the folding fan was brought from China by Portuguese traders and soon spread to neighboring Spain and Italy. At first these Oriental curiosities induced the development of folding fans which were quite distinctive in form and construction. In Italian paintings of the late 16th century we find evidence that a type of fan, now known to students and collectors as a duck's foot, was favored in Italy. This type was quite small and had eight ivory sticks, round in section with ball finials. The seven panels between the sticks were very narrow and had a concave top, so that when the fan was fully extended it formed a quarter-circle with the rounded panels having the appearance of the webs between a duck's toes. The panels themselves were composed of alternate strips of vellum and mica decorated with floral or geometric painted patterns.

Mica, a silica crystal which splits readily into thin, transparent, and very flexible plates of various colors, was a popular medium for early European fans. In some cases the panels were entirely of mica, delicately painted to simulate the appearance of stained glass, but more often it was combined with strips of vellum. Conversely, mounts were also made entirely of vellum which was cut in intricate geometrical patterns, not unlike the paper doilies of modern times with their fine, lacy appearance. This technique, known as decoupage or decoupé, appears to have originated in Italy and then been perfected in France, from whence it spread to England in the closing decade of the 16th century. A celebrated example is preserved in the Cluny Museum and has a vellum mount cut in a pattern of lozenges and circles into which tiny pieces of mica have been inserted. Decoupage became something of a craze in refined circles, even kings and queens practicing their skills.

Whereas Chinese fans paid little attention to the sticks, from the outset European makers appreciated that these elements could be things of beauty in their own right. As they became larger and flatter, so they came to be decorated, first by carving, fretting, chasing, or piercing in plain ivory and later embellished with gold or silver inlays. There was also a penchant for sticks of contrasting colors and materials, ivory alternating with

Right: Princess Marie Anne Victoria, the future wife of King Joao I of Portugal, painted after Largilliera in 1733 when she was age 12. By this time it had become de rigueur to portray royal ladies with a fan in their hand.

mother-of-pearl, horn, tortoiseshell, or polished hardwoods. It was not long before a wide range of brisé fans, emulating the styles of China, were also being produced in Portugal, Spain, Italy, and France, from where they spread northward to Germany and the Low Countries, and eventually to England and Scandinavia. The use of fans was still largely confined to court circles, although gentlemen as well as ladies carried fans, a custom that endured for two centuries.

Before the end of the 16th century Paris emerged as the leading center for the manufacture of fans in Europe. The origins of the Guild of Fan makers, formally instituted by Louis XIV in March 1673, could be traced back to a decree of Henri IV in 1594 according the makers of fans certain rights and privileges. Various edicts from 1664 to 1678 laid down rules and regulations for the proper conduct of the manufacture and trade in fans. In 1673 the guild had 60 members; by the middle of the 18th century their number had risen to 150 master fan makers, probably employing many hundreds more in their workshops. This phenomenal increase would probably have been much greater, but for the revocation of the Edict of Nantes in 1685 which drove Protestants and Nonconformists out of France. Many of them took refuge in England and introduced a wide range of technologies in glass, silver, furniture, and other aspects of the applied and decorative arts. Fan making was one of the industries brought over the English Channel at that time and by 1709 it was so well established that the Fan makers' Company was then formed. It is interesting to note that, in order to protect this infant industry, the importation of fans from India and China was then prohibited for a number of years.

Every type of folding fan was produced in France, but among them the brisé fan predominated in the 18th century. Ivory was the preferred medium, although horn, bone, tortoiseshell, and hardwoods were also used. Like their Oriental counterparts, great attention was paid to the fretting and piercing of the blades to simulate fine lace and great skill was imparted to

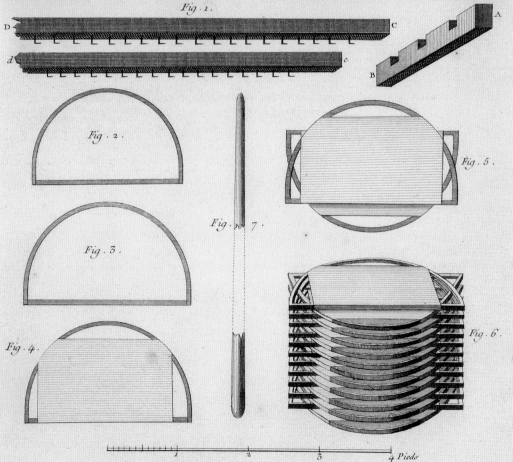

Left: One of the plates from "*Le Travail de l'Eventailliste*" in the *Encyclopedie of Denis Diderot* (Paris, 1765), a stage in the production of fans. There are vignettes at the top of each plate illustrating typical scenes from the fan maker's workshop. The plates show the preparation of sheets of paper and the method of glueing them to form the fan leaves, and — as here — the intricate processes involved in the mounting of the fan leaves.

Right: An engraving of 1795 showing fashionable ladies of the period carrying folded fans.

Left and Above: A late-18th century print showing a Venetian lady displaying her fan in coquettish mood.

Pag. 73.

Tom. 2

Venitienne

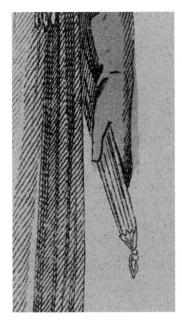

Right and Above: A fashion plate of about 1805, showing the high-waisted Directoire style of day dresses. Both ladies, of course, are carrying their fans.

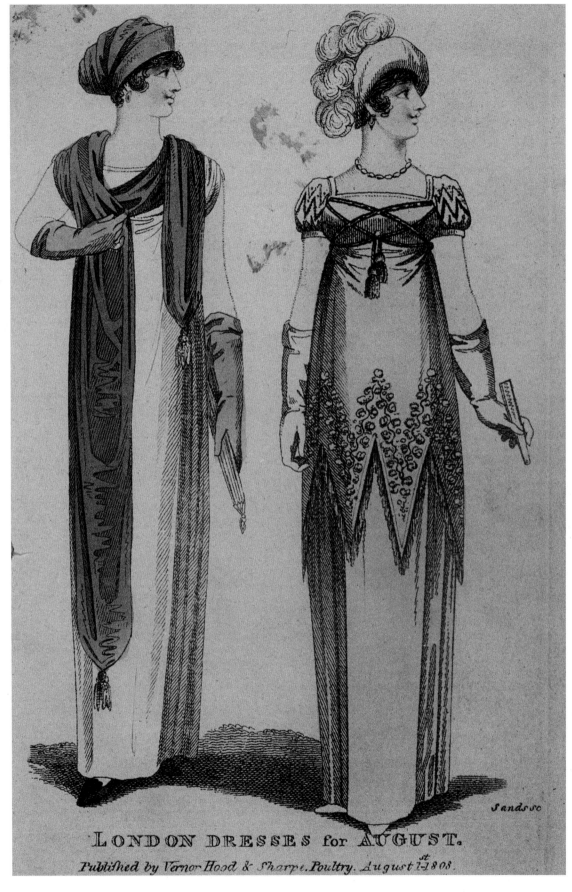

LONDON DRESSES for AUGUST.

Published by Vernor Hood & Sharpe. Poultry. August 1st 1808.

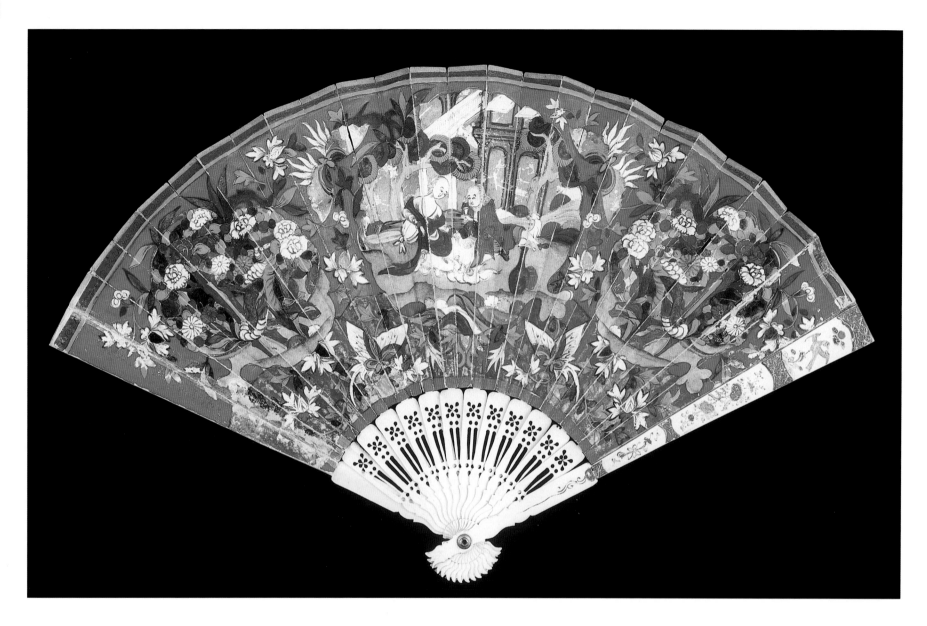

Above: A rare miniature mica fan dating from the late 17th century and painted with European lovers in a landscape.

Above: The elegant embarkation scene
on the recto of this fan — dating
around 1700 — may possibly depict the
Queen of Sheba. The verso features a
peacock and other exotic birds.

Two fans from the early 18th century. The upper fan, with mother-of-pearl sticks, shows a painted scene of the paradise of the gods while the lower one, dating around 1720, depicts the triumph of Alexander. Classical scenes of this kind were immensely popular throughout the 18th century.

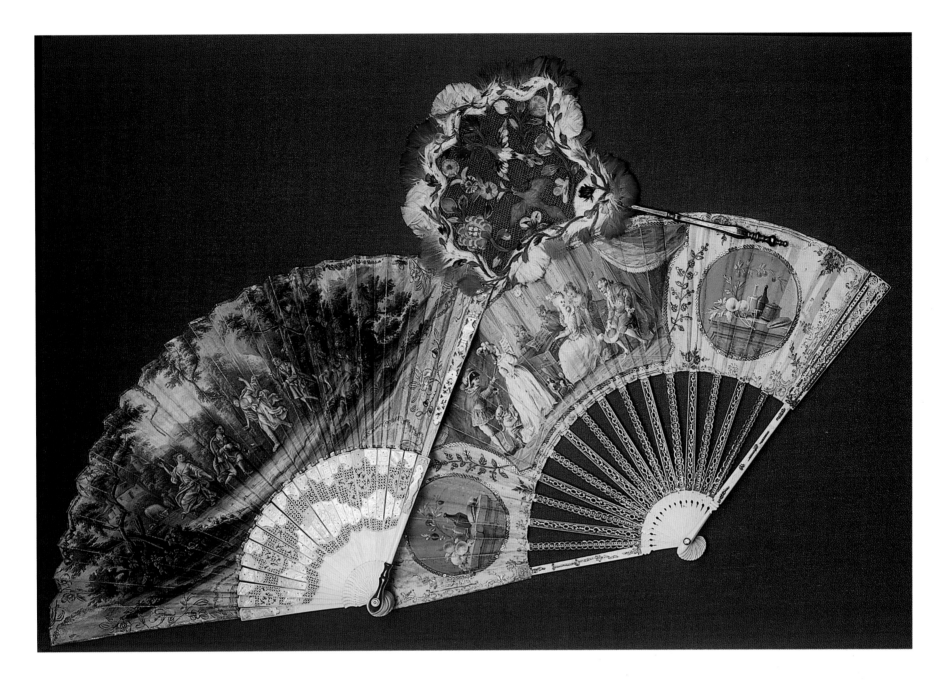

Above: Three 18th century fans: (left) an English fan of about 1730 with a single classical scene; (center) a South American handscreen; and (right) a French fan of about 1775, with a central vignette flanked by two smaller scenes in cartouches.

the linking of the sticks at the top by means of special silk ribbons. At the same time, fans gradually became larger and eventually extended to the full semicircle, the number of sticks increasing at the same time. The broad ivory blades were exquisitely painted in oils by hand, using the same techniques as those of contemporary portrait miniatures but with the far greater scope afforded by the fan opened to its fullest extent; indeed, there was a brief fashion in England for ivory brisé fans decorated with medallions containing portrait miniatures. In general, however, these beautiful fans

depicted genre and pastoral scenes and landscapes while classical compositions were also very popular.

From about 1740 onwards painted fans were often finished in a type of varnish known as "vernis Martin" which imparted a hard, glossy surface not unlike Oriental lacquer. Of course, fans were only one class of object which was subjected to this treatment, though it probably attained its finest flowering in this medium. In fans of this type lacquer was applied mainly to unpierced ivory sticks.

Left: A group of six fans, mainly French, produced between 1720 and 1730.

Right: A collection of 18th century fans:

1 An ivory brisé fan of about 1720, painted and lacquered, with Bacchus and Ariadne on the recto. The verso depicts a merchant and his lady with a boy attendant on a quay with a ship and fortress in the background.

2 An ivory brisé fan of about 1720, painted and lacquered with Zeus, Hercules, Ceres, Bacchus, Mercury, Apollo, and other gods banqueting. The verso depicts two figures in a garden, flanked by vignettes of putti. The lower third of the fan is covered with portraits.

3 An ivory brisé fan of the early 18th century, painted and lacquered with a classical feast on the recto and a river scene on the verso.

4 An ivory brisé fan of the early 18th century featuring Pan and Syrinx, the guardsticks carved with the portrait of a lady.

5 An early 18th century pierced ivory brisé fan, painted with a double portrait of a royal couple flanked by circular landscapes. The leaf is decorated with

spangles in the form of crowns and flowerheads while the lower end of the sticks is painted with chinoiserie.

6 An early 18th century fan with a painted leaf showing figures dancing beside a palace, the verso depicting a spray of flowers. The ivory sticks are carved and pierced with figures.

7 A very rare early 18th century fan with a painted classical scene. The ivory sticks are carved and pierced with serpentine shapes and scallop shells and clouté with carved mother-of-pearl and piqué with silver.

8 An early 18th century ivory brisé fan, painted and lacquered on both sides, with a series of vignettes of figures in landscapes.

Above: An early 18th century ivory brisé fan, painted and lacquered on both sides, with a series of vignettes of figures in landscapes.

Pages 64–65: An unmounted fan leaf of 1727, the center etched in outline and illuminated in watercolor, body color, and gold, showing the Coronation banquet of King George II.

Above: An Italian fan of about 1725 with a painted leaf of chicken skin showing the eruption of Vesuvius and a group of Neapolitan fishermen watching the spectacle. Fans of this kind were popular mementoes of the Grand Tour.

In the third quarter of the 18th century the minuet fan was developed, similar to the brisé fan but somewhat larger, with sticks of carved or fretted bone or ivory, displaying a large central vignette when unfolded. These vignettes were hand-painted after the manner of such fashionable artists of the period as Poggi, Bartolozzi, Cipriani, or Boucher. By the end of the century, however, the technique devised by Bartolozzi for reproducing polychrome pictures by means of a form of stippled printing, originally confined to paper prints, had been applied to fans, so it is important to be able to distinguish hand-painted originals from the later (and much cheaper) printed versions.

Left: A small black lacquered fan with lettering "Long Live the King" picked out in gold spangles. It was produced as a souvenir of the Coronation of King George II in 1727.

Right: A rare English commemorative fan of 1728; below the classical scene the ivory sticks are inscribed THE ROYAL FAMILY and bear finely engraved portraits of King George II and Queen Caroline of Ansbach.

Below left: A fine lace fan of about 1730, the leaf of point d'Angleterre worked with a fountain of Cupid riding a swan.

Between about 1800 and 1840 sandalwood and cedar supplanted ivory as the preferred medium for brisé fans; at the same time, the quality of the carving and fretting tended to deteriorate. On the other hand, the range of subjects depicted was now much larger, though mainly in the neo-classical style. Both hand-painted and printed fans were produced, the latter being much more numerous. To this period also belongs the rare double-image brisé fans whose blades reverse to produce four different

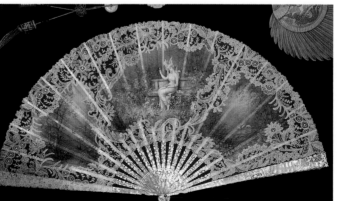

Top row, far left: The verso of a north Italian fan of the early 18th century, painted with vignettes of elegant musicians and castles, with mother-of-pearl sticks.

Top row, left: An English fan of about 1740 with a painted leaf showing bird-catchers and shepherdesses beside a well (recto).

Bottom row, far left: Venus, the goddess of love, was a very popular subject for fan leaves. This small fan, dating about 1730 shows the "Toilet of Venus," with medieval figures in the reserves.

Bottom row, left: A printed fan with a hand-colored etching of an allegorical scene, believed to symbolize the Treaty of Aix la Chapelle in 1747. The desirability of such fans is enhanced by their strong historical interest.

Right: An English fan of about 1742 depicting a view of Cheltenham well from the southeast. Although unsigned, it is known to have been painted by Thomas Robins the Elder. Topographical fans of this kind are rare and much sought after on account of their interest to local collectors.

pictures in all. The heyday of this type was the 1820s and as they were very expensive to produce it is not surprising that they are ranked very highly by present day collectors.

The expulsion of large numbers of French Huguenot craftsmen in the wake of the revocation of the Edict of Nantes in 1685 spread the delicate art of fan making to the Netherlands, Germany, and England. The Dutch probably came closest to the French in the production of brisé fans of the highest quality, but it is impossible to generalize, and many splendid examples of English origin have also been recorded. An indigenous fan industry slowly developed in England from the middle of the 16th century. Tudor and Stuart fans were made of vellum, cut and pierced to simulate lace like those then being produced on the Continent. Very few fans of the period before the Civil War are now extant, and most of these are in museum collections. These early fans are not as finely made or attractive in design as their French or Italian counterparts but are of immense rarity.

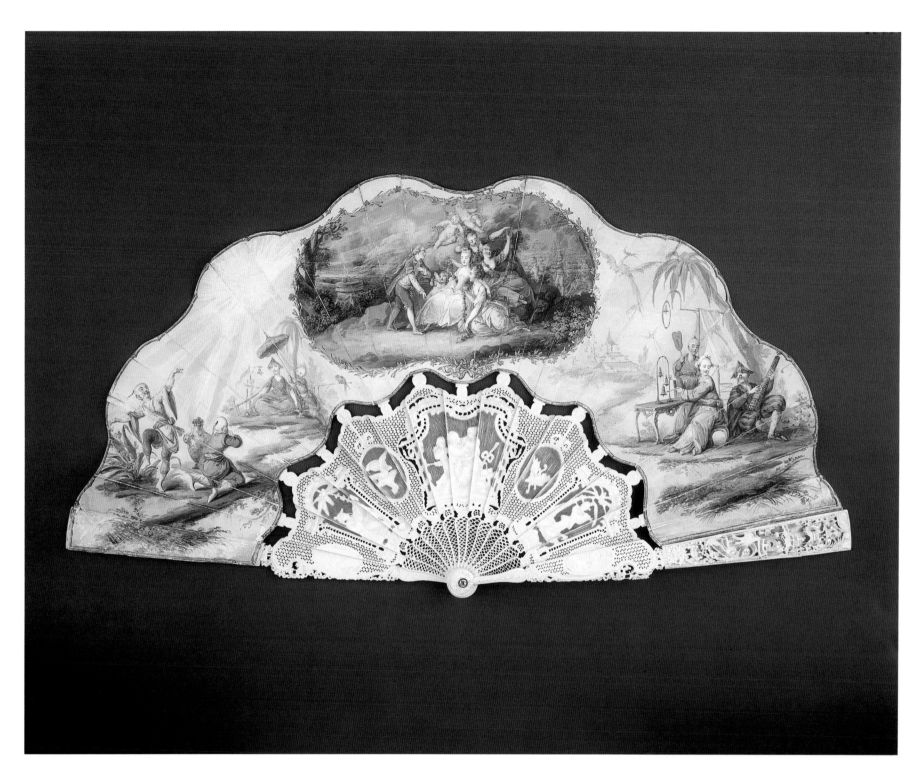

Painted fans came into fashion in Britain following the restoration of the monarchy in 1660. English fans of the ensuing 15 years had an arc of 140 to 160 degrees, with 14–18 shouldered sticks, covered by the fan leaf to a depth of about two-thirds. The quality of the painting and subject mat- ter varies enormously, and while the best examples are now very expen- sive, fans of this period with relatively crude brushwork are generaly much cheaper. After the influx of Huguenot refugees, many of whom settled in the Soho and St. Giles districts of London, the quality of painted

Above, left and right: A superb French fan of about 1750, the scalloped leaf painted with lovers in the manner of Pillement on the recto (above), while the verso (above right) depicts Chinese

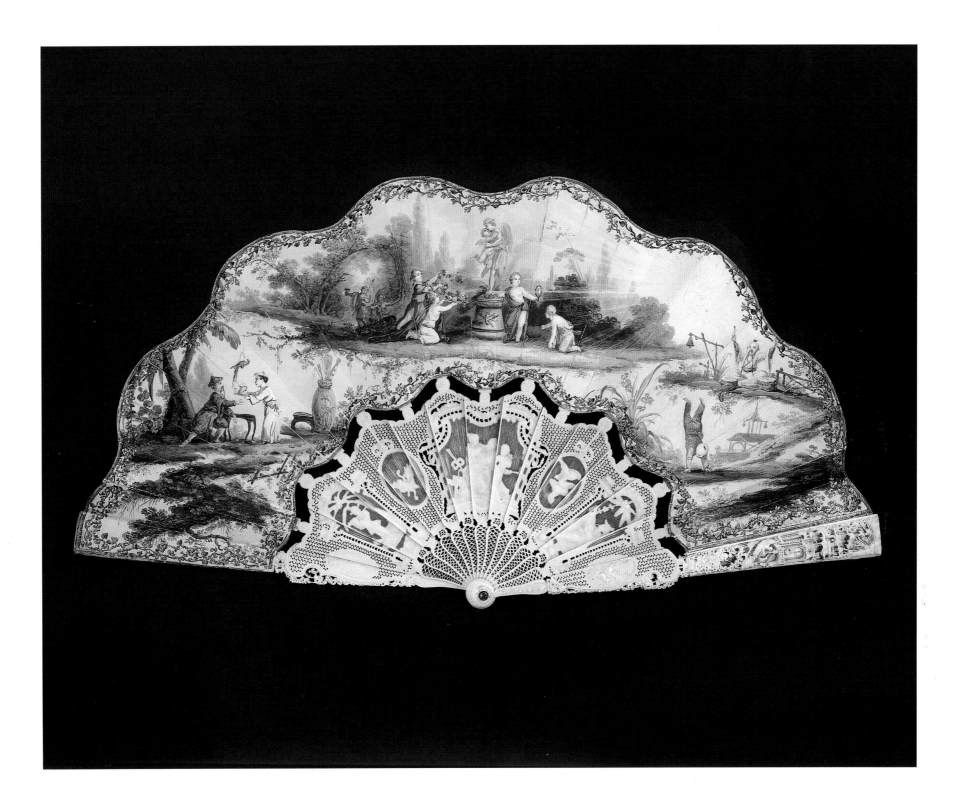

and European children. The ivory sticks are finely carved with lovers, while the guardsticks are decorated with chinoiserie buildings and figures.

fans improved enormously. At the same time, the size and shape of fans increased; between 1690 and 1730 the number of sticks averaged 24–26, but thereafter it decreased again, to 18–21. After 1730 sticks became longer, but mounts became shorter, reflecting the prevailing fashion in

France where the techniques of piercing and fretting were extended to the exposed parts of sticks, combined with fan leaves with painted scenes and vignettes. This type of fan, combining the two main techniques of decoration, became larger in the second half of the 18th century, by which time

Left: A selection of eight mid-18th century fans, including a rare Jacobite fan (lower right), the leaf possibly painted by Sir Robert Strange. It bears a fine portrait of Prince Charles Edward Stuart — "Bonnie Prince Charlie" — above elements of the three kingdoms and female allegories of Ireland, England, and Scotland.

Right: A selection of eight fans from the middle of the 18th century, showing a wide variety of decorative treatment of the ivory or mother-of-pearl sticks, as well as the range of painted scenes, from classical and allegorical compositions to contemporary landscapes.

the arc had increased to 180 degrees or even more. The shoulders gradually disappeared and between 1750 and 1770 the ornament was complete on each individual stick. Thereafter, sticks were decorated in such a way that the ornament spread right across the entire range, and this permitted a wide range of techniques including carving, painting, staining, chasing, piercing, and lacquering. The motif appeared across two, three, or four sticks at

Above: A mid-18th century English fan depicting the Roman goddess Juno, protectress of women, watching over a childbirth scene.

74

Above: An English fan of about 1752 painted after Canaletto with a view of Ranelagh Gardens, Chelsea and showing the Chinese pavilion in the foreground.

first, and gradually extended to the entire ensemble. In the course of the 18th century the use of vellum, parchment, and other materials derived from the skins of chickens, pigs, and kid goats gave way to silk or paper.

Sometimes small silk vignettes were printed on silk and applied to the silk mount, painted over by hand. Paper mounts were decorated with gouache but, as the century wore on, there was a tendency to incorporate

Left: A selection of six mid-18th century fans. The fan (upper left) is English and dates from 1753, illustrating "the new game of Piquet now in play among different nations," possibly also a satirical reference to the politicking in Europe which led eventually to the outbreak of the Seven Years' War in 1756.

Right: A fan of Dutch or Flemish origin, dating around 1760, showing a Biblical scene of Rebecca and Eliezer at the well, the sticks of bone pierced and gilt.

Far right: A fan of French or German origin produced about 1760 which once belonged to Queen Marie of Romania. The painted leaf has a shaped vignette of lovers by the altar of love, flanked by oval vignettes showing a boy building a house of cards and two portrait miniatures of ladies under mica, the reserves painted with urns on plinths and busts on pillars. The ivory sticks are carved, pierced and gilt.

Right: An intriguing French topographical fan about 1760 showing an animated street scene with a mobile theater on the left and a human pyramid on the right. The architecture and landmarks would help to identify the exact location.

Above: A fan of about 1760 whose painted leaf shows a fairground scene. The ivory sticks are carved, pierced, silvered and gilt with figures.

Above: An important mask fan of about
1760, the leaf painted in the form of a
clown's face with the eyes and mouth
cut out. The shaped vignettes at the
sides depict elegant couples dining and
dancing.

Below: A fan of about 1770, the silk leaf painted with a blue urn of flowers flanked by birds perched in trees. The sticks are decorated with gold and lacquer.

Above right: A fine articulated fan, probably from south Germany, about 1770, the silk leaf painted with a central vignette of an elegant family, flanked by two smaller vignettes.

Right: An articulated French fan of about 1775, the silk leaf painted with putti aiming arrows at lovers beside the altar of love.

additional ornament in the form of spangles or straw-work. Pastoral scenes continued to predominate, although from about 1760 scenes from Ravenet, Watteau, and Boucher were also immensely popular.

The 18th century was the golden age of the European fan, and in particular the period from about 1750 to 1790 witnessed the most sumptuous, costly, and downright extravagant fans ever produced. Craftsmen vied with each other in the intricacy and delicacy of the carving and piercing of ivory and mother-of-pearl, while the sticks and guards were embellished with gold, silver, cloisonné, enamels, and even precious stones. These costly bibelots are now of the greatest rarity, so many of them, like their erstwhile owners, having perished during the French Revolution.

In the 1760s there developed a craze for a type of fan which came to be known as a "cabriolet," an allusion to the light two-wheeled vehicle introduced to Paris in 1755 by Josiah Child. These carriages took Paris by storm and inevitably inspired new shapes in the applied arts, from furniture to fans. Cabriolet fans had mounts in two or more separate concentric sections, hand-painted or engraved with vignettes which often showed people riding in cabriolets. Apart from their unusual form and decorative features, these fans are now much sought after by collectors specializing in the theme of transport.

Fans decorated with general scenery and landscapes are still fairly plentiful, while those depicting identifiable landmarks are much sought after on account of their topographical or architectural interest. Even more desirable are fans whose motifs have a topical flavor. In this category come the fans showing ballooning. After the pioneer ascents by the Montgolfiers, Pilâtre de Rozier, Charles, Robert, Blanchard, and Lunardi in the 1780s, aerostation became all the rage and infected all manner of objects, from chairbacks to bonnets and watch-cases; but undoubtedly the ballooning craze found its greatest flowering in the fans of the closing decades of the 18th century. These balloon fans were invariably etched and colored by hand.

The 1780s till about the middle of the 19th century, however, was the heyday of the printed paper fan. Although engravings, often colored by

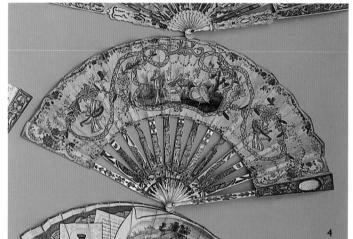

1 An Italian fan of about 1775, formerly in the collection of Martin Willcocks, with a trompe l'oeil of turkeys and fruit, music, a manuscript, ribbons, and watercolors of Etruscan vases.

2 An amusing French fan of about 1775 showing a gentleman and two ladies beside a wheel of fortune, closely observed by Cupid. The reserves depict urns containing bouquets of flowers decorated with spangles, and the mother-of-pearl sticks are carved, pierced and gilt, while the guard sticks are set with oval miniatures of putti under mica.

3 A Dutch fan of about 1775 with a painted leaf showing two elegant couples in a formal garden, flanked by chamfered rectangular motifs and trailing floral ornament. This fan is very unusual in having a signature — W. Struyk — most are unsigned.

4 A French fan of about 1775, the silk leaf painted with four elegant musicians and the reserves decorated with flowers worked in chainstitch and embroidered in sequins. The mother-of-pearl sticks are carved with musicians, pierced, and gilt.

5 A French fan of about 1775 showing four elegant musicians in a park, the reserves decorated with charming chinoiserie vignettes with a trompe l'oeil of fans and objects trimmed with sequins.

Above: Although Madrid later became a major center of fan manufacture, many Spanish fans of the late-18th century were produced in Paris. This is a splendid example, made doubly interesting by its panoramic view of the great siege of Gibraltar by the Spanish fleet in 1779, which helps to date it fairly precisely.

hand, had been used in fan leaves from the early years of the century, this medium really came into its own in the turbulent period which led up to the French Revolution in 1789 and carried on well into the following century. What the printed fans of the late 18th and early 19th centuries lacked aesthetically and technically was amply compensated for in their vigorous social and political character. Like the satirical cartoon, with which they had much in common, they became a popular propaganda medium. Political

figures were lampooned, and even royalty was not spared. Victories in the French Revolutionary and Napoleonic Wars were celebrated, plays and popular songs publicized, and doggerel verse savagely attacked personalities and factions alike. These topical fans were rather ephemeral and, though cheap at the time, are now highly elusive as the vast majority would have been discarded soon after they were produced. Although they reached their zenith at the turn of the century, they continued to be an

Left: A group of European fans dating around 1780, including (upper left) an Austrian fan showing the catechism of love, a scene from *The Beaux Stratagem* by Farquhar with a German translation of the lyrics printed alongside.

Right: A group of five late-18th century fans, including three with hand-painted landscapes, a magnificent brisé fan (upper left), and a very unusual Dutch fan (upper right) showing a balloon under construction. The majority of ballooning fans show the balloons in flight.

Left: A group of three Italian chicken-skin fan leaves of about 1790 which have been mounted in glazed semi-circular frames for wall decoration. As a rule, these frames have a straight bottom, but the lowest of the three has an unusual frame shaped in order to accentuate the panoramic view painted on the leaf.

Right: A group of three Italian chicken-skin fan leaves dating from 1770 to 1785, mounted in more conventional rectangular frames. The hand-painted vignettes depict various views of Vesuvius and the Bay of Naples, a perennially popular topic.

1 An Italian fan of about 1780 with a central vignette showing Athena and her attendants, flanked by two small cartouches depicting buildings in the Campagna, the reserves decorated with Pompeian ornament.

2 An English fan of about 1780 with three oval stipple engravings printed in color on silk, the reserves painted with two tiny still lives of wine, fruit and cheese. The mother-of-pearl sticks are pierced, silvered, and gilt.

3 An English chicken-skin fan of about 1780 with a central vignette of three kittens amidst Pompeian decoration and the crowned monogram of Louisa, Countess of Aylesford. The scenes may have been painted by her husband, the fourth Earl, better known as the land-scape artist and etcher Heanage Finch.

4 An English fan with a silk leaf bearing three stipple engravings of Hobbinol and Candaretta by Petro Williams Tomkins after Gainsborough, and Venus presenting Helen of Troy to Paris, after Angelica Kauffman. The ivory sticks have been painted with simulated jasper plaques, pierced, and gilt.

5 A pierced ivory brisé fan of French origin, with a central vignette showing an allegory of marriage, and believed to depict the Prince of Wales (later King George IV) marrying Mrs. Fitzherbert in 1786 before Religion and Hymen, with

side cartouches featuring Fidelity and
Constancy.

6, 7 Two Italian fans of about 1780 with
hand-painted leaves depicting St. Peter's
in Rome, with carriages in the foreground. The value of these rare topographical fans is enhanced by their
transport interest.

8 A Roman chicken-skin fan of about
1780 with a hand-painted scene of the
Falls at Tivoli from the Temple of the
Sibyl, the temple itself being depicted
on the verso. The ivory sticks are
carved and pierced with a motif of a
stag at bay and other hunting scenes.

Above right: An unusual French printed
fan of 1793 showing a hand-colored
etched map of Central America with the
route of the proposed canal across
Nicaragua to link the Atlantic and
Pacific oceans.

Right: An Italian fan of about 1800, the
leaf painted with a banquet of gods and
heroes, including Hercules and Neptune.
The verso has vignettes of musicians
and castles.

Left: A group of fans dating from the beginning of the 19th century, including two ballooning subjects (bottom) and genre subjects such as "The Fortune Teller" and "The Meet," a hunting scene signed by Rene Valette.

Right: A French chinoiserie painted fan
of about 1820 showing figures in a
gazebo, above an Art Nouveau fan,
signed Reyor for Ernest Kees, showing
three handmaidens, about 1900.

Left: Three unmounted fan leaves (top to bottom): "Eau de Cythere," French, 1890; a canepin leaf of about 1875; and a canepin leaf of about 1865. Both hand-painted and chromolithographed leaves of this period delighted in genre scenes such as these, replete with detail.

Above: A fine fan signed by Edouard Moreau and dated 1865. From about this period more and more fan leaves were signed and dated, adding considerably to their interest. This fan depicts a French skating scene of the 16th century.

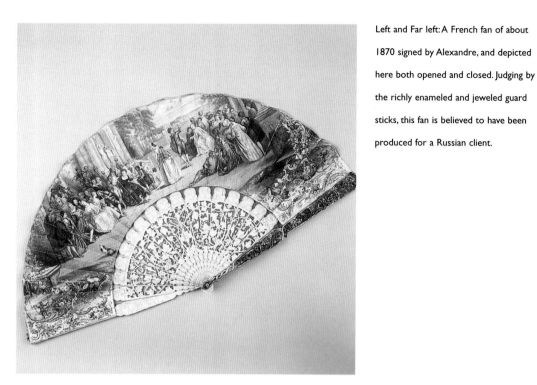

Left and Far left: A French fan of about 1870 signed by Alexandre, and depicted here both opened and closed. Judging by the richly enameled and jeweled guard sticks, this fan is believed to have been produced for a Russian client.

important medium for popular dissent as late as the 1840s. Crude they may have been in manufacture, but these fans have a dramatic immediacy that transcends their shortcomings.

There were printed fans of English manufacture depicting scenes from the Bible. As ladies were expected to carry fans to church it was only right and proper that these should depict suitable subjects for religious contemplation. Distinctive fans were also produced for weddings, funerals, and periods of mourning, the last-named in somber hues with allegories of grief. Fans recounting the salient dates in English history were designed for the use of young ladies in colleges and seminaries, and fans giving details such as the structure of a flower, with naming of parts, were produced for the same purpose.

Although the French Revolutions swept away all that was elegant in the Ancien Regime, fashion again became paramount during the Napoleonic era. The fans of the First Empire, however, were a pale shadow of the glories of the 18th century, generally smaller with plainer sticks and mounts of gauze decorated with spangles and tinsel. To this period belongs the lorgnette fan, with broad sticks of fretted ivory or horn into which were

Right: A selection of fans produced in the 1870s, the leaves with their scenic vignettes and miniature portraits all signed by G. Prodoscini, although the mother-of-pearl sticks were by Jorel.

Left: A French fan of about 1875, the leaf painted with fruit and game in the manner of Jan Fyt, the verso with monogram DD, by Jorel.

Below left: A French fan with mother-of-pearl sticks of about 1878 showing a staghunt after the chase painted by Ol. de Penne.

Right: Richard Doyle, the celebrated caricaturist and book-illustrator, also experimented in the restricted medium of the fan leaf. This whimsical scene is light pastel shades, was painted about 1880.

Following page: Recto and verso of a rare canepin leaf fan showing Diana and gods with a temple scene, painted by Pater Carl Fabergé, the Russian Court jeweler, about 1885.

set tiny glass lenses which enabled the holder to observe others without herself being observed. In some cases the glass was set in the handle, so that the closed fan could be reversed and used as a quizzing glass. Despite the debasement of the fan for political reasons, it continued to hold its own as a fashion accessory right through to the end of the 19th century and even beyond. It was still an indispensable accessory in Edwardian times, but

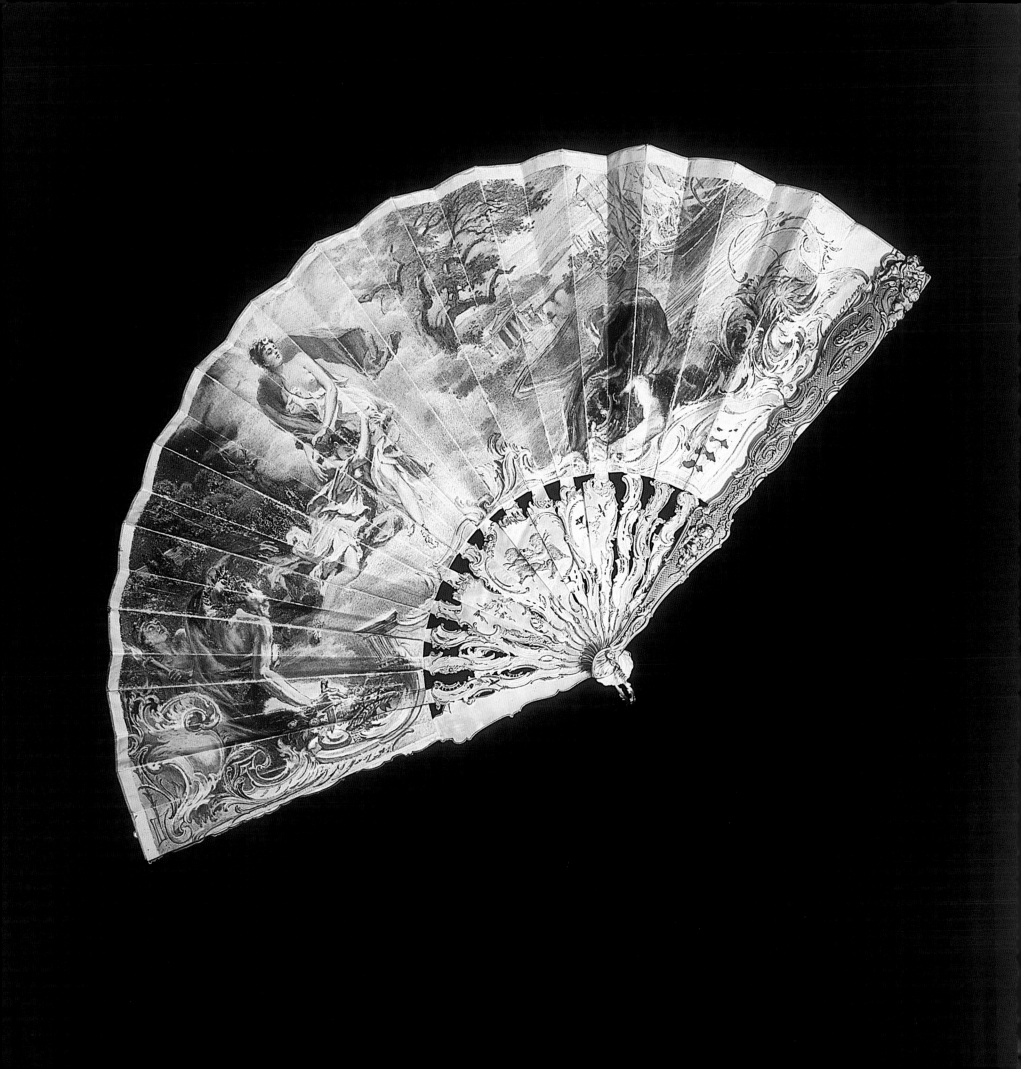

like so many other aspects of costume it vanished from the scene during the First World War. After the vogue for political and satirical fans had run its course, paper fans continued to be produced for commemorative purposes. Pictorial printed paper fans were a popular souvenir of the great fairs and exhibitions of the 19th century, notably the Great Exhibition of 1851, the Centennial Exposition at Philadelphia in 1876, the Exposition Universelle in Paris in 1878, the Columbian Exposition at Chicago in 1893, and many lesser events of a similar nature; such exhibition fans constitute a quite distinct branch of the hobby.

From about 1860 to the end of the 19th century, ladies' fans were usually fitted with silk mounts, which may be found with hand-painted or printed scenes, either extending over the entire leaf or divided into two or

Left: Autograph fans were briefly in fashion in the late 19th century. This fine example bears the signatures of over 80 musicians and composers and appears to have been assembled around the turn of the century.

Right: A selection of six fans from the late-19th century, including a fine scene of the Seville Fair of 1888, painted by Ussel (bottom right).

Left: A selection of late-19th century fans including a portrait of Johann Strauss II, Albert Smith's ascent of Mont Blanc and "Au Soulier de Cendrillon" signed by G. Lasellaz.

Right: A splendid example of a French advertising fan dating from about 1900. The chromolithographed fan, produced on behalf of the Chemins de Fer de l'Ouest, has views of Rouen, the Casino of Dieppe, and Dinard.

three vignettes separated by ornamental frames. Many different techniques were applied to the ornamentation of these silk fan leaves, including embroidery, appliqué, and the use of spangles and metallic thread.

Over a rather longer period (1840–1910) there was a resurgence of interest in Chinese fans, with the difference that these were entirely European in manufacture, even if their motifs were consciously modeled on Chinese originals. These chinoiserie fans often reproduced motifs which had, in an earlier period, been popularized through the medium of *famille verte* and other forms of Chinese porcelain, but the majority of these 19th century fans made extensive use of feathers, either in their natural state or painted, with bird motifs decorating the center. In the same way, the mandarin fan came back into popularity, though here again most of the examples dating between 1860 and the First World War were actually produced in France or Britain. They ranged widely in style and quality. At the upper

Left: A selection of eight fans all dating from the end of the 19th or beginning of the 20th centuries, showing how the basic motifs of fans had remained more or less unchanged for several generations. Note the variety of shapes and styles as well as the range in sizes.

end of the scale they were every bit as fine as the Chinese originals, with painted ivory faces and clothing embroidered in applied silks; but many of them used proto-plastic materials, such as erinoid and parkesine, as a cheap substitute for ivory.

Although lithography had been invented at the end of the 18th century, it was not widely used in the manufacture of paper fans until the middle of the 19th century, and enjoyed a certain popularity in the late Victorian period when chromolithography (a form of multicolor printing which, at its best, was noted for the rich warmth of its colors) reached its peak. Cheap printing was allied to mechanical techniques in carving sticks, devised by Alphonse Baude in 1859, which robbed them of all that was best in traditional craftsmanship.

Reaction against the flood of cheap factory productions in the ensuing decade prompted a revival of fan making as a hand craft. It is significant that fans were highly regarded by the Arts and Crafts Movement and the Aesthetic Movement that followed, both being strongly influenced by the fans of China and Japan. In the 1860s there were various attempts to revive hand-made fans, and these efforts culminated in two great fan exhibitions, staged in Paris and London, in 1870. Among the painters who produced designs for fan leaves in the closing years of the 19th century may be cited Pierre Bonnard (1867–1947), John Lewis Brown (1829-90), Edgar Degas (1834–1917), Maurice Denis (1870–1943), Georges de Feure (1868–1928), Jean-Louis Forain (1852–1931), François-Louis François (1814–97), Paul Gauguin (1848–1903), Ludwig von Hoffman (1861–1945), Max Liebermann (1847–1935), Edouard Manet (1832–83), Giuseppe de Nittis (1846–84), Camille Pissarro (1830–97), Paul Signac (1863–1935), and Theophile-Alexandre Steinlen (1859–1923).

Most of these artists used the medium of the fan leaf to produce miniature versions of the work they had previously brought to a much larger canvas, and their pleated fan leaves were in the orthodox semicircular format; but Alfons Mucha (1860–1939), the dancing dervish of the curving line and high priest of the Art Nouveau style, produced rigid fans in which the leaf described almost a full circle and was attached to a handle with concentric circular motifs. These creations, however, belong more to the realm of fine art, in which the fan was merely a vehicle for individual paintings, and they appear to have had little or no influence on contemporary trends in commercial fan production.

At their best, the chromolithographed paper fans of the 1890s and the Edwardian era, with rural scenes and floral decoration, are very attractive and are consequently much in demand; but many of them were quite tawdry, and it is important to discriminate between the exquisite and the mediocre. So much of European and American fan design at the turn of the century was third-rate, ephemeral fans without the redeeming feature of the earlier political or souvenir fans. They might have hastened the decline of the fan in everyday use, had not the First World War and the sweeping social changes that came in its wake sounded the death knell. Although there had been some paper fans in the mid- and late-19th century with patriotic motifs, inspired by such conflicts as the American Civil War (1861–65), the Franco-Prussian War (1870–71), the Spanish-American War (1898), and the Anglo-Boer War (1899–1902), it is perhaps significant that the much greater cataclysm of the First World War did not inspire much in the way of fans. The fan was a symbol of a more tranquill, elegant age, and the grim atmosphere engendered by the "war to end all wars" was certainly not conducive to anything so gay and light-hearted as these trifles.

Fans did not disappear overnight as a result of the First World War. They lingered on fitfully throughout the inter-war years and, indeed, there were attempts to revive them from time to time. They survive to this day but mostly in the form of rather cheap and tawdry tourist souvenirs, their sticks of molded plastic and mounts of printed nylon; useful for cooling oneself on the Costa perhaps, but unlikely ever to be taken seriously as a fashion accessory. There have also been brave attempts in very recent years to revive the fan as art object, and since the early 1980s artists such as Manuel Baptista in Portugal, Klaus Basset in Germany, Miriam Schapiro in Canada, and Margie Hughto in the United States have achieved notable success in this medium.

Left: A montage of fans which range from Chinese and European chinoiserie fans of the mid-18th century to the early 20th century. The later fans include a printed fan of about 1910 featuring can-can dancers and two advertising fans of the 1920s.

Left: A truly remarkable fan, hand-painted in 1928 and signed by Marin Marie (the pen-name of Marin Durand Coupel de Saint-Front, 1901—87). It depicts the Bermuda-rigged racing schooner *L'Aile VI* owned by Madame Virginie Heriot (whose monogram VH also appears on the fan). It was presented to her by the Yacht Club of France in 1929. The fan leaf is decorated with classical motifs including Amphitrite and dolphins. Its enormous value is enhanced by the fact that the artist was himself a renowned single-handed transatlantic yachstman.

the *language* of fans

4

So far we have examined the role of the fan as a cooling device, with subsidiary functions as fly-swatter or fire-bellows, but there was another role which, as the years passed, gradually assumed the dominant position—the fan as the supreme instrument of silent communication.

Holding a fan gave you something to do with your hands; down the centuries, mankind has always felt awkward without something in the hand to fiddle and toy with, and nothing ever surpassed the fan as an object which became virtually an extension of the hand and, as such, an indispensable adjunct of body language. This applied to small fans of any kind, although the folding fan in its many guises was the ideal implement. Even when closed, it could be held in one or both hands, the fingertips of one hand playing lightly along the top while the movement of the swiveled foot was controlled by the forefinger and thumb of the other.

A well-balanced fan could be made to perform all kinds of tricks. In the hands of a gentleman a closed fan might be held languidly one moment and used the next in a jabbing motion to emphasize a point. A large fan with lavish filigree or piqué (ornament by means of tiny silver rivets) on the heavy ivory guards might make a capital weapon with which to strike an opponent in a fit of temper, although no self-respecting gentleman, far less a lady of course, would ever dream of doing such a barbaric and ill-mannered thing.

None the less, there are sufficient numbers of well-attested incidences to show that the fan, as the nearest weapon to hand, was sometimes used in anger. The iron fans of Japan, used essentially as battle standards, could also be extremely efficient weapons in close-combat fighting.

Right: While the gentlemen give their rapt attention to the girl at the piano, the young lady in the foreground sits back languidly with her fan fully extended, in this narrative engraving of 1880 simply entitled "Listening."

Previous page: Early 18th century fan (see page 62).

Left: The actress known as the "Jersey Lily," one-time mistress of the future King Edward VII and society beauty, Lillie Langtry (1852–1929) is shown in a ball gown and tiara, carrying a fine lace fan.

Right: In this portrait by Nemo of Victoria, eldest daughter of Queen Victoria and wife of Frederick III of Germany, published by *Vanity Fair* in 1884, the subject carries a closed fan with an extravagant tasseled strap.

Inevitably the ubiquity of fans demanded that there should be rules and regulations governing their use. These rules might be unwritten but they were very real all the same. In China, for example, there was a strict dress code concerning the fan which depended on the weather and the season of the year. It was considered very bad form to produce a fan before spring turned to summer with a corresponding raising of the temperature. One day not a fan would be in sight; the very next, as the temperature began to soar, fans would suddenly appear out of nowhere as if by some pre-arranged signal. At first, only rigid fans would be socially acceptable, but when the weather became really hot, folding fans came into their own, pre-ceding stretched fans and, finally, feather fans which were produced in the third month of summer. Presumably there also came a day when the temperature cooled and fans were hidden away once more as winter drew on.

Interestingly, there seems to have been a similar convention in Europe. In his *Reflections and Anecdotes of the Queen of Sweden*, the Encyclopedist Jean la Rond d'Alembert recounts how some ladies of the Court asked Queen Christina if it would be permissible for them to carry fans in winter as well as summer. Christina, who had no time for such idle fripperies, responded with the cutting remark, "Fans! What do you want with fans? You're fantastic enough already!" In the French text there is a pun linking *éventails* (fans) with *eventées* (fantastic). The ladies apparently took their revenge by carrying fans at all times and on every occasion thereafter, regardless of the weather or the season. In this strange manner the habit of carrying fans all the year round rapidly spread to all other parts of Europe.

The Chinese and Japanese also had various rituals concerning the actual use of the fan, in religious observance and in every aspect of daily life. There were ways of holding fans, opened or closed, when meeting social equals, or when people of different classes met and conversed. The most extreme form of this arose when two mandarins of equal rank encountered each other as they rode in their palanquins. They would remain seated in the shadows and shout across to each other from behind fans

Left: The fan as the sine qua non of royalty of all kinds is exemplified in this photograph of Lydia Kamerera Liliuokalani, Queen of Hawaii, on her throne in Honolulu, 1888. Polynesian by birth and upbringing, she was thoroughly westernized by American missionaries and would have appreciated the absolute necessity of always carrying a fan.

held up to cover their faces like masks. So if there is any truth in the story of how the fan originated during the Feast of Lanterns, it may be said that in this ritual the fan had come full circle.

It was in Europe, however, that the use of the fan was developed to the highest degree, to the extent that entire conversations could be conducted without a single word actually uttered. It must be supposed that the various gestures and signals, combined with the use of the hands and the position of the fan in relation to the face or the body, gradually evolved over a very long period, and that in polite society various conventions eventually emerged which were readily understood. It was in Spain, a

Right: Queen Victoria, in the year of her Diamond Jubilee (1897), is shown here pensively toying with her fan. It appears to be an all-black fan, perhaps an indication of her on-going mourning for Prince Albert.

Following spread: Sarah Bernhardt is seen using the fan effectively to enhance a dramatic pose in a scene from *La Tosca* by Victorien Sardou, photographed by W. and D. Downey in 1890.

country whose climate made the fan indispensable at most seasons of the year, that the language of the fan was first codified by a writer named Fenella in the early 18th century. This was translated into German by Fray Bartholomäus and thence into French. The leading French fan maker, J. Duvelleroy, produced an English version which was extensively quoted by George Wooliscroft Rhead in his *History of the Fan*, published in 1910.

Octave Uzanne has left us a fascinating account of the fan, which was translated into English in a limited edition in 1884. Not only did he make acute observations regarding the habits and customs associated with fans

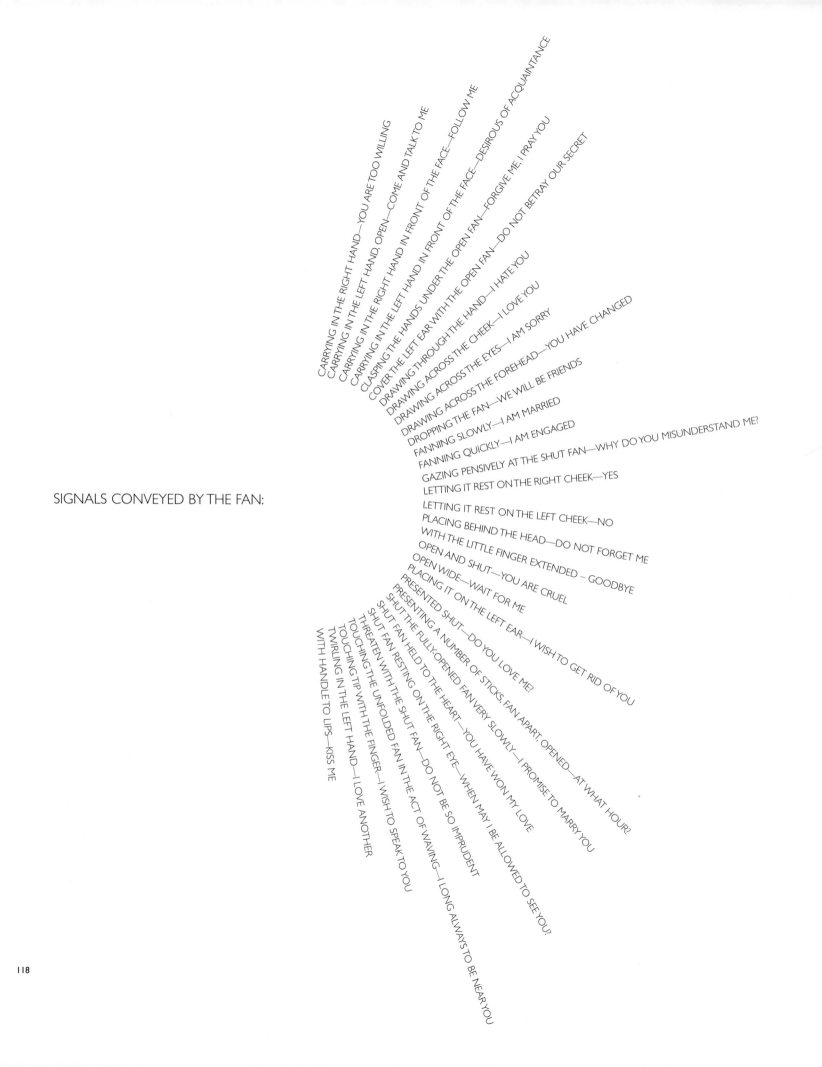

SIGNALS CONVEYED BY THE FAN:

CARRYING IN THE RIGHT HAND—YOU ARE TOO WILLING
CARRYING IN THE LEFT HAND, OPEN—COME AND TALK TO ME
CARRYING IN THE RIGHT HAND IN FRONT OF THE FACE—FOLLOW ME
CARRYING IN THE LEFT HAND IN FRONT OF THE FACE—DESIROUS OF ACQUAINTANCE
CLASPING THE HANDS UNDER THE OPEN FAN—FORGIVE ME, I PRAY YOU
COVER THE LEFT EAR WITH THE OPEN FAN—DO NOT BETRAY OUR SECRET
DRAWING THROUGH THE HAND—I HATE YOU
DRAWING ACROSS THE CHEEK—I LOVE YOU
DRAWING ACROSS THE EYES—I AM SORRY
DRAWING ACROSS THE FOREHEAD—YOU HAVE CHANGED
DROPPING THE FAN—WE WILL BE FRIENDS
FANNING SLOWLY—I AM MARRIED
FANNING QUICKLY—I AM ENGAGED
GAZING PENSIVELY AT THE SHUT FAN—WHY DO YOU MISUNDERSTAND ME?
LETTING IT REST ON THE RIGHT CHEEK—YES

LETTING IT REST ON THE LEFT CHEEK—NO
PLACING BEHIND THE HEAD—DO NOT FORGET ME
WITH THE LITTLE FINGER EXTENDED – GOODBYE
OPEN AND SHUT—YOU ARE CRUEL
OPEN WIDE—WAIT FOR ME
PLACING IT ON THE LEFT EAR—I WISH TO GET RID OF YOU
PRESENTING A NUMBER OF STICKS FAN APART, OPENED—AT WHAT HOUR?
PRESENTED SHUT—DO YOU LOVE ME?
SHUT THE FULLY-OPENED FAN VERY SLOWLY—I PROMISE TO MARRY YOU
SHUT FAN HELD TO THE HEART—YOU HAVE WON MY LOVE
SHUT FAN RESTING ON THE RIGHT EYE—WHEN MAY I BE ALLOWED TO SEE YOU?
THREATEN WITH THE SHUT FAN IN THE ACT OF WAVING—I LONG ALWAYS TO BE NEAR YOU
TOUCHING THE UNFOLDED FAN IN THE ACT OF WAVING—DO NOT BE SO IMPRUDENT
TOUCHING TIP WITH THE FINGER—I WISH TO SPEAK TO YOU
TWIRLING IN THE LEFT HAND—I LOVE ANOTHER
WITH HANDLE TO LIPS—KISS ME

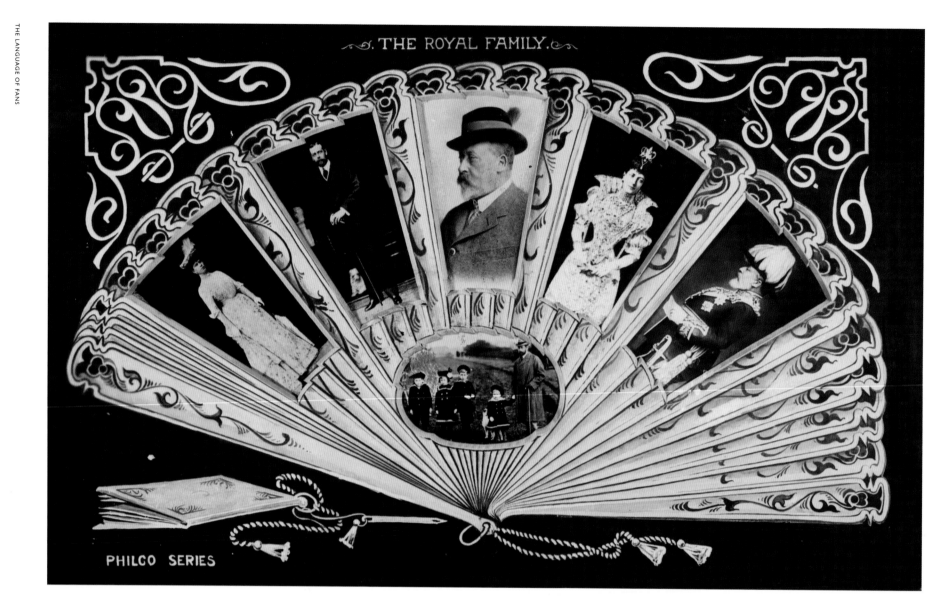

in various countries, culled from earlier writers, but he also trawled through the novels, poetry and belles-lettres of the major European countries in search of references to fans which shed light on the manner in which they were employed as well as people's attitudes to them. Describing lorgnette fans at some length, he comments on the fact that Parisian ladies habitually used them when discreetly peeping on the men bathing nude in the Seine at the Porte Saint Bernard. The lorgnette fan also came into its own at the opera or theater when it was used by both sexes to appraise each other. Such fans were very popular with the ladies, it seems, because they afforded them an opportunity to weigh up the gentlemen without compromising themselves. Uzanne's chatty book may be of little use in charting the technical and aesthetic development of the fan, but it is an invaluable source of gossip and anecdote regarding the use or misuse of the fan, especially in the higher echelons of French society on the eve of the Revolution. His book is a virtual anthology of the verse, occasionally witty and elegant, sometimes stilted and florid, with which lovers accompanied gifts of fans to the ladies they were courting. There were stereotyped conventions which described the fan as a weapon of "the cruel fair" or as a bellows to beat up the flames of love and passion. One is left with the impression that flirting with fans was an occupation that took up an

Left: A picture postcard by Philco reproducing a souvenir fan with portraits of
King Edward VII and Queen Alexandra
as well as other members of the British
royal family, probably as a souvenir of
the coronation of 1902.

Right: The Lady Elizabeth Bowes-Lyon,
later Queen Consort of King George VI
and now Queen Mother, photographed
at her Scottish home, Glamis Castle.
Lady Elizabeth was eight years old at
the time, but even little girls (in high
society at any rate) carried fans.

inordinate amount of time, energy and intellectual exercise at the French Court. He cites Madame D'Aublay who stoutly defended the fan when a gentleman of her acquaintance disparaged it as a thoroughly useless toy. On the contrary, she opined, it was the most useful accoutrement any lady could wish, "occupying the hands, giving the eyes something to look at, and taking away stiffness and formality from the figure and deportment." When the man argues that the real use of the fan is to hide "a particular blush that ought not to appear," she counters that such action would only tend to draw attention to the blush. The man remains unconvinced, arguing that in such circumstances the fan served to distract attention: "it may be done under pretence at absence—rubbing the cheek or nose, putting it up accidentally to the eye—in a thousand ways."

This usage was confirmed by another of Uzanne's sources, the Baronne de Chapt, from whose philosophical writings he extracted the following advice:

"It is so pretty, so convenient, so suited to give countenance to a young girl, and to extricate her from embarrassment when she presents herself in a circle and blushes, that it cannot be too highly exalted. We see it straying over cheeks, bosoms, hands, with an elegance which everywhere produces admirers. Thus a citizeness sort of person, who is but so-and-so, according to the slang of the day, in wit and beauty, becomes supportable if she knows the different moves of the fan, and can adapt them to the right occasion. Love uses the fan as an infant a toy, makes it assume all sorts of shapes; breaks it even, and lets it fall a thousand times to the ground. How many fans has not love torn! They are the trophies of his glory and the images of the caprices of the fair sex!

"It is not a matter of indifference a fallen fan. Such a fall is ordinarily the result of reflection, intended as a test of the ardour and celerity of aspiring suitors. They run, they prostrate themselves, and he who picks up the fan first, and knows how stealthily to kiss the hand that takes it, carries off the victory. The lady is obliged for his promptitude, and it is then that the eyes in sign of gratitude speak louder even than the lips."

Left: For evening wear a large feather fan was considered the height of fashion in Edwardian times, as this fashion plate of 1911 indicates.

Right: Although fans for everyday use were going out of fashion in the 1920s, they were still a requisite of certain occasions. In this photograph of 1921 a hawker is shown selling fans to ladies in cars lining up for admission to a royal garden party.

Left: American actress Norma Shearer (1902–83) is shown in this photograph of 1925 wearing a close-fitting evening dress and holding a large feather fan.

Right: Marlene Dietrich, shown in a scene from *Le Patriote* (The Mad Emperor) in January 1938. Large feather fans remained in vogue for formal evenings until the outbreak of the Second World War.

Left: Even after the Second World War, small fans might still be carried to formal evening functions, as this photograph of October 1947 indicates.

Right: An evening gown being modeled
at a Paris fashion show in February
1953. The model is carrying a feather
fan, although by that date such acces-
sories were seldom carried.

Left: Fans might no longer be in evidence at balls and banquets, but they continued as a useful accessory when modeling elegant evening dresses, such as this scene from Christian Dior's autumn-winter collection in Paris, August 1953.

Similar passages occur early on in English literature as well. Sir Richard Steele, in the *Tatler* of 4 August 1709, publishes an imaginary letter from a spinster named Virgetta. To her young friend Delamira, on the eve of the latter's wedding, she writes urging her to give up various "excellences" in her conduct, including "that inexpressible beauty in your manner of playing your fan," whereby she had made so many "Conquests and Triumphs." Steele uses this as a vehicle to poke mild fun at the various conceits and contrivances associated with the fan which he likens to a weapon, constantly used in the battle of the sexes:

"You may observe in all publick Assemblies the sexes seem to separate themselves and to attack each other with Eye-shot; that is the time when the Fan, which is the Armour of Woman, is of most use in her Defence; for our minds are constructed by the waving of that little instrument, and our thoughts appear in Composure or Agitation according to the Motion of it."

His fellow essayist, Joseph Addison, writing in the *Spectator* two years later, developed the theme. In his eyes the fan was not so much a defensive implement but a weapon, commenting, "Women are armed with Fans as Men are with swords and sometimes do more execution with them."

"There is an infinite variety of motion to be made use of in the flutter of a Fan. There is the angry Flutter, the modest Flutter, the timorous Flutter, the confused Flutter, the merry Flutter, the amorous Flutter. Not to be tedious, there is scarce any emotion of the Mind which does not produce a similar agitation of the Fan; inasmuch if I only see the fan of a disciplined Lady I know very well if she laughs, frowns or blushes. I have seen a fan so very angry that it would have been dangerous for the absent lover who provoked it to come within the wind of it. And at other times so very languishing that I have been glad for the Lady's sake the lover was at a sufficient distance from it. I need not add that the Fan is either a Prude or a Coquette according to the nature of the person who bears it."

With a view to ensuring that "ladies may be entire mistresses of the weapon which they bear," Addison proposed establishing an academy where young women would receive proper training, "according to the most fashionable airs and motions that are now practised at court." He goes on, in a series of amusing metaphors, to describe the rigorous drills and maneuvers, after the manner of military manuals of the period, including such orders as "Handle your fans!", "Unfurl your fans!", "Discharge your fans!", "Ground your fans!" and "Flutter your fans". He was confident that "by the right observation of these few plain words of command, a woman of tolerable genius, who will apply herself diligently to her exercise for the space of but one half-year, shall be able to give her fan all the graces that can possibly enter into that little modish machine." Lest he be accused of sexism, Addison proposed to admit young gentlemen to his fan academy that they might be taught the art of "gallanting a fan." He had "reserved little plain fans made for this use, to avoid expense."

Apart from a wide range of gestures and positions for holding the fan to convey various signals and emotions, there was even a systematic method of signaling precise messages, in much the same fashion as, in a later era, men might transmit and receive signals by Morse code. An artless poem in *The Gentleman's Magazine* in 1740, reproduced by Rhead, describes the conversation fan. Rhead goes on to explain in some detail how the fan was used in a form of semaphore. Omitting the letter J, the alphabet was divided into five groups of five letters. By the permutation and combination of movements—fan in left hand to right arm, right hand to left arm, against the bosom, raising it to the mouth or forehead—an elaborate series of 25 different movements could be generated. Reading this account, one is left with the inescapable conclusion that it must have been tedious and time-consuming, although dexterity borne of constant practice may have enabled two adept practitioners of the art to carry on a dialogue in

Left: American students wearing academic dress at their graduation ceremony. The girl on the left is holding a lace fan, perhaps reflecting the fact that in hot weather in the Southern states a fan is still very necessary.

Left: Fashion designer Karl Lagerfeld holding a fan although, as a fashion (for men at any rate), carrying fans does not appear to have caught on.

much the same way as deaf mutes communicate. It must also be assumed that this system was practiced only by ladies, as one cannot imagine that men, no matter how gallant or skilled in courtly manners, would have the time or patience for such an elaborate ritual. This semaphore was reproduced on cheap printed fans of the late 18th and early 19th centuries. Known as the "Fanology, or the Ladies Conversation Fan," it was devised by Charles Francis Badini and marketed commercially by William Cock of Pall Mall on and after 7 August 1797, to judge by the imprint on the fan itself. There is an air of male superciliousness about the inscription in the lower cartouche in the centre of the leaf which promised that "This Fan improves the friendship, and sets forth a plan For Ladies to Chit Chat and hold the Tongue." On either side of the central panel the capital letters and their corresponding numerals were printed across the top, while underneath appeared copious instructions for use. This fan was unusual in being entirely printed by letterpress, and devoid of any pictorial element other than a rather crude sketch of Venus wresting the bow from Cupid. Alongside appeared a quatrain:

The telegraph of Cupid in this fan
Though you should find, suspect no wrong;
'Tis but a simple and diverting plan
For ladies to chit-chat and hold the tongue.

The term "telegraph" alluded to the recent invention by Claude Chappe of a system of relaying signals quickly over long distances which greatly accelerated communications during the French Revolutionary Wars.

Perhaps the most important part which the fan ever played was in the play which launched Oscar Wilde's brilliant but brief career as a dramatist. *Lady Windermere's Fan* (1892) must be second only to Yorick's skull as the most important prop in the history of the theater. As the indispensable article of fashion, without which no self-respecting lady would have appeared in public, the fan was then at its zenith. It is sad to ponder that within a decade Wilde would be dead, in disgrace, and the fan itself beginning to go out of fashion. Wilde has long been rehabilitated but for many years now the fan has been regarded only as an object of curiosity and antiquarian interest.

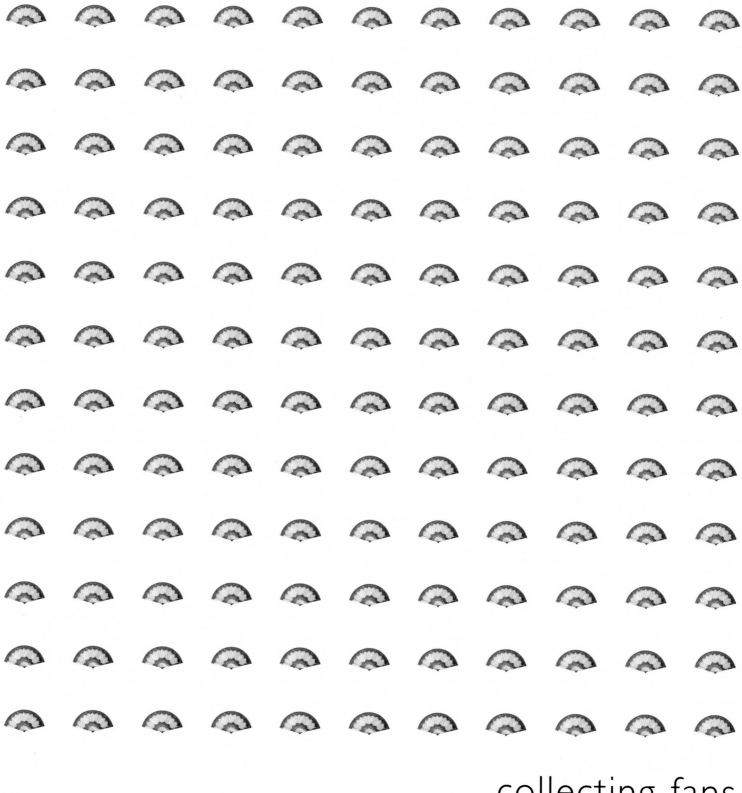

collecting fans

5

Fan collecting was well established centuries ago in China where the leaves were prized as fine examples of painting and calligraphy. As previously mentioned, the leaves were often dismounted and preserved in albums. Western fans, on the other hand, were more usually kept intact on account of the decorative features of the sticks and guards. Thus there was immediately a dichotomy between Occidental fans, which remained essentially three-dimensional objects, and Oriental fans, which were two-dimensional. This made the latter easier to collect and store in a practical form, whereas the former, kept intact, were much more of a problem.

The best-quality fans were sold in cases specially manufactured for the purpose and were usually kept in these cases when not actually in use. The cheaper fans were sold uncased and were probably discarded when they began to show evidence of wear and tear, the mount became detached from its sticks, or the leaf otherwise sustained damage. Folded fans, in particular, suffered inevitably from a weakening of the mount along the pleats; unless they were dismounted in the Chinese fashion and stuck into albums or affixed to boards, they would sustain damage in the long run.

Like so many articles in everyday use, the fan was something which people tended to take for granted. The idea of appreciating a fan for its own sake, intrinsically or aesthetically, does not seem to have arisen in Europe, at least not to any real extent, before the middle of the 19th century, and only then because the golden age of the fan as a true object of vertu was long past. Interestingly, for a subject so closely associated with the fair sex, many of the greatest collectors of the past were men. Sir Augustus

Right: The fans of the 18th and 19th century are often very colorful with classical scenes.

Previous page: English 18th century fan (see page 67).

Wollaston Franks of the British Museum was an avid collector in the 19th century and many of his finest pieces passed into the hands of Robert Walker, whose cabinet of antique fans was sold at Sotheby's in 1882. Sir Matthew Digby Wyatt, one of the great pioneers of industrial design in the mid-19th century, formed an impressive collection which he bequeathed to the Victoria and Albert Museum, with which he was closely associated from its earliest days. In Germany, the other country where Fan collecting was prominent, the leading authority on antique fans was the industrialist Marc Rosenberg, whose collection was displayed at the exhibitions in Karlsruhe (1891) and Madrid (1920). Nearer the present time the finest collection of Oriental fans was that formed by Leonard Messel which passed to his daughter, the Countess of Rosse, and which was the subject of exhibitions at the Victoria and Albert Museum in 1967 and 1978.

To redress the balance, however, it should be noted that arguably the finest collection of fans of all types ever formed by a single collector was that built up between about 1830 and 1890 by Lady Charlotte Schreiber (1812–95). Intelligent, single-minded, and above all, having both the time and the money to pursue her hobby, she kept meticulous records of her many expeditions in pursuit of the finest fans and fan leaves. These she eventually distilled into two volumes dealing with English and foreign material and published in 1888 and 1890 respectively. The following year she gave her vast collection to the Department of Prints and Drawings at the British Museum and this, in turn, resulted in the encyclopaedic catalog of her collection, compiled by Lionel Cust and published in 1893. Both George Woolliscroft Rhead (1910) and MacIver Percival (1920) drew heavily on the Schreiber Collection in the compilation of their own books,

Above: An important collection of 18th century fans, on view before sale at Christie's South Kensington, London in June 1991.

138

Above: An interesting group of French fans from the 1780s. The upper two have satirical subjects from the revolutionary period.

both of which have stood the test of time and are still indispensable reading, although Rhead is a bibliophilic rarity and even Percival's *Fan Book* is very elusive. The fact that it never ran to a second edition reflects the fact that, by the time it was published, fan collecting was suffering from a post-war decline.

If fan collecting was in the doldrums in Europe from 1920 onwards, the emphasis rapidly shifted across the Atlantic. The fan industry in America had been relatively small, and most of the fans used there were imported from England or France. Collecting objects of the past was much more widespread at all levels of society in the United States, perhaps due to the fact that people had proportionately more surplus disposable income and also more time to pursue a hobby. At any rate, as fan collecting declined in Britain and Europe, it expanded in America where many of the largest collections of more recent times were formed. A revival of interest in fans as collectables in the years following the Second World War led to the formation of the Fan Circle in 1975, today the largest society devoted to fans and fan leaves, with a worldwide membership.

The market in antique fans peaked in the 1880s when Charlotte Schreiber and Robert Walker were only the front-runners among a coterie of wealthy enthusiasts. Prices fell sharply during and after the First World War and were still very depressed when the Second World War came along. As late as the 1960s there was little market in Britain for old fans, a deplorable situation which was shared by old lace. Since then, of course, both subjects have risen sharply in price as the market has hardened. The sterling propaganda work of the Fan Circle, together with a number of prestigious exhibitions, has created a much greater awareness of fans at all levels. Significantly the number of museums that now boast a comprehensive collection has risen, and what is more important, they now display their collections in a much more imaginative fashion than was once the case. At one time individual fans or small collections might occasionally feature in the salerooms but nowadays there are specialist sales devoted to them, matched by catalogs which are beautifully illustrated in color, with excellent descriptions, making them useful reference works of permanent value.

Many collectors of the present generation appear to have started with one or two examples of 19th century English or French fans inherited from a grandmother or great-aunt and, intrigued by their subject matter or composition, were drawn to other items which they came across while browsing in antique shops or perhaps attending a country-house sale. My good friend, the late Martin Willcocks, was a stamp dealer all his working life but he became a keen devotee of fans, originally through admiring the engraving and lithography on old printed fans, techniques which were analogous to the production of stamps, and from this initial interest he eventually graduated to the realm of the painted fan which he quite rightly regarded as a minor branch of the fine arts.

Some collectors of fans are drawn to them for purely antiquarian or romantic interest as fascinating objects of a long-vanished elegance; others,

like Martin Willcocks, are attracted to them for technical reasons and derive much pleasure from researching the designs and the methods of construction. A singular feature of European painted fans is that very few of them were signed by their painter, far less dated. Those examples which have come to light are all well documented for that very reason, but this leaves in limbo the vast majority which may have been painted after the manner of Fragonard or Watteau but which have never yet been proven to have come from the brushes of these masters, despite wishful thinking in many old-time sale catalogs. Only the art fans from the late 19th century onward have born the signatures or initials of the artists. It has to be conceded that the vast majority of the painted fans of earlier times were produced in workshops, often on what was virtually an assembly line, and while the subjects may have been derived from paintings by famous artists, they were merely copied. In some cases elements of a well-known painting were lifted out of context and grouped together to fit the fan leaf.

Printed fans, on the other hand, are both easier to identify and often more challenging as a result. An Act of Parliament in 1735 decreed that printed fans in England had to bear the publisher's name and the date of manufacture. This has encouraged collectors to study the output of particular publishers such as Gamble at the sign of the Golden Fan, or the Cock family. Even in the case of fan leaves in which the printer's details were trimmed off in order to fit the sticks, it is often possible to attribute a fan on account of characteristics in the printing or coloring. In recent years, moreover, a great deal of research has been carried out, checking commercial directories and contemporary newspapers for the advertisements of fan makers, and thus the background to fan production has gradually been built up. Both Rhead and Percival provided alphabetical lists of known fan painters, printers and designers in their books but a much more detailed and comprehensive listing will be found in Bertha de Vere Green's *Fans Over the Ages* (1975).

It is impossible to suggest to people what they should collect; this is a matter best left to personal predeliction. Obviously there are certain

classes of fan whose prices are now prohibitive. You would have to be pretty well-heeled to consider collecting fans featuring ballooning and other early forms of transportation, far less the gold and bejeweled fans of the mid-18th century. The printed paper fans of the late 18th century, especially those with political overtones, are also very expensive in fine condition, their very ephemeral nature having rendered them highly elusive. But this still leaves broad areas, from Oriental imports to 19th century engraved, lithographed, and hand-colored fans. While many collectors are content to pick up whatever takes their fancy, others concentrate on topographical fans pertaining especially to their own county or region. Fans were also produced as "premiums" or advertising giveaways and these, too, are now attracting serious attention.

When considering a potential purchase there are various factors which should be taken into consideration. Unusual decorative features on the sticks and the pinion holding them together inevitably command a good premium, all other things being equal. The use of piqué or filigree work is a major plus factor. Fans with personal associations with historic personalities can be worth very much more than their style and quality might generally warrant, but in such cases everything depends on their provenance.

A subject which is attracting increasing attention is the cases in which good quality fans were housed. The earliest cases were lined with velvet and covered with shagreen or dark leather. Some 18th century fans have original papier-mâché boxes complete with the shop label. After about 1720 boxes had red or green covers with silver mounts or gilt patterns. Silver mounts were sometimes hallmarked up to 1790, but after that date they were exempted on grounds of size. Fans with the original cases rate a good premium. Later cases often have the manufacturer's name and trademark in gilt lettering on a white satin lining. Occasionally, however, dealers in the past were tempted to marry a good fan to a case which was not the original, thereby enhancing the sale price of the two together. Nowadays both dealers and collectors are far more knowledgeable than they were 30 years ago, but one should still be on guard, especially in the case of fans which come up for sale in provincial auctions.

The condition of a fan is of paramount importance, and those which have been damaged or carelessly repaired can be heavily discounted. This applies particularly to fans with mounts of silk or gauze. A rough and ready method of repair, when sticks were damaged, was to glue the broken one to its neighbor, but this spoils the symmetry of the picture when the fan is extended. Fan leaves may often be found without their matching sticks and even in this condition they are still quite collectable, although their value will be considerably reduced.

Rather more problematical are old sticks with more recent mounts. This may have been done quite legitimately, as fashions changed or a damaged or worn fan leaf was replaced by a later one, but still intended for actual use. The problem is that, at this remove in time, it is often very difficult, if not well nigh impossible, to distinguish between a genuinely contemporary replacement and one that was carried out in relatively recent times, cannibalizing fan leaves which had been detached from the original sticks and marrying them to sticks whose original leaves were beyond repair. Much easier to detect is the mounting of early leaves on sticks of a much later date. Sometimes technical features can be of assistance. For example, a metal loop was attached to the pinion from about 1816 onwards, for threading with ribbon. The presence of this feature on a fan with an 18th century mount would immediately render it suspect.

Sooner or later collectors are faced with the problems of cleaning or repairing fans. This situation may arise when old fans are discovered in attics or cellars, or are turned up in old trunks full of the detritus of the past. When considering what to do in these circumstances I am forcibly reminded of the advice given by Punch to men contemplating matrimony: "Don't!" Countless fans have been irremediably damaged as a result of well-intentioned but misguided cleaning or botched repairs, and there is no more heart-breaking sight. If you feel that you must clean a fan which has got heavily impregnated with the dust and grime of the centuries, do not under any circumstances use detergents, hot water, or any abrasive materials or metal polishes. Toilet soap, lemon juice and lukewarm water, soft rags, cotton-wool balls, cotton buds, and wooden cocktail sticks are the only equipment you will require, plus a great deal of tender, loving care. Begin by cleaning the guards with the fan closed and only then progress to the individual sticks and finally the fan leaf itself. If in doubt, leave it out; be gentle at all times and take care not to rub off original varnish or paint. Some collectors swear by the various patent products designed to clean and polish piano keys as ideal for treating dirty or discolored ivory on fans, but I would be very loath to recommend anything quite so drastic.

Similarly I would urge the greatest caution when it comes to cleaning the mount itself. Silks and lace are so fragile that they might well disintegrate if you tried to clean them, and the same holds good for chicken skin and other fine types of leather. The best advice would be to take your problem pieces to your nearest museum where staff are skilled in handling

materials of all kinds. The same remark applies to the repair of damaged fans, invariably a job for a skilled restorer; remember, if you buy a rare fan in damaged condition it may cost you more in the long run to have it restored than it would have been had you bided your time until a perfect example turned up. Some collectors of long-standing are adept at touching up the color on mounts where it has become faded. This is a highly skilled task and while it doubtless gives immense satisfaction to those who have the necessary expertise and patience, again it is not something I would recommend anyone to embark on without some degree of training.

The biggest headache in restoring folded fans is tears and splits along the folds. Occasionally one comes across an old fan which may have lain undisturbed for generations. It looks lovely, but as soon as you open it the leaf begins to crack. Even opening such a fan is a hazardous operation and once fully extended it should be preserved in that state. The backs of folds which have been weakened or cracked, can be reinforced by narrow strips of rice paper or pieces cut from a light-colored nylon stocking, using a clear gum applied by a watercolour paintbrush. This is a very fiddly job and not something to be undertaken lightly. Faded or frayed ribbons are unsightly and should be replaced by narrow china ribbons although these are becoming much harder to find nowadays.

Finally, as regards housing your collection, opinions, and tastes vary widely. I have seen very attractive displays of fans or fan leaves mounted on a dark baize and then framed for wall-hanging, but a word of warning: do not hang such frames in a room where they will be exposed to direct sunlight. In fact, even diffused sunlight can do an amazing amount of harm to delicate colors, especially the gouache and watercolors used for so many fans. Shallow boxes large enough to hold a fan fully extended are probably the simplest solution, and for this purpose large chocolate boxes are ideal provided that the fans are wrapped individually in chemically inert tissue or soft muslin. If you are lucky enough to possess a fairly large collection then you are probably also wealthy enough to afford a proper cabinet to house your treasures. The type with shallow drawers used for housing maps and draftsmen's plans is excellent, preferably the all-metal variety, as not all timbers are chemically inert. Remember that sunlight and atmospheric pollution are your worst enemies, but it is also important to keep your collection in a room without undue variations in temperature and humidity. This may sound off-putting, but it really boils down to common sense and, at the end of the day, you will have the satisfaction of knowing that you are able to pass on your collection to the next generation in as good a condition as you acquired it.

Recommended Reading

Alexander, Hélène: *The World of the Fan*; Preston, 1976.

Anquetil, Marie-Amelie: *Éventails de Maurice Denis*; Paris, 1983.

Armstrong, Nancy: *A Collector's History of Fans*; London, 1974.

Armstrong, Nancy: *The Book of Fans*; New Malden, 1979.

Baro, Carlos M. and Escoda, Juan: *Éventails Anciens*; Lausanne, 1957.

Brinker, Helmut: *Zauber des chinesischen Fächers*; Zurich, 1979.

Catalani, Carla: *Waaiers*; Bussum (Netherlands), 1966.

Chiba, Reiko: *Painted Fans of Japan*; Tokyo, 1962.

Collins, Bernard Ross: *A Short Account of the Worshipful Company of Fanmakers*;
    London, 1950.

Cust, Lionel: *Catalogue of the Collection of Fans and Fan Leaves presented to the
    Trustees of the British Museum by the Lady Charlotte Schreiber*; London, 1893.

Dorrington-Ward, Carol (ed.): *Fans from the East*; Boston, 1978.

Fan Guild: *Fan Leaves*; Boston, 1961.

Flory, M. A.: *A Book about Fans*; London, 1895.

Gostelow, Mary: *A Collector's Guide to Fans*; Dublin, 1976.

Green, Bertha de Vere: *A Collector's Guide to Fans Over the Ages*; London, 1973.

Hay, John: *An Exhibition of the Art of Chinese Fan Painting*; London 1974.

Henderson, Milne: *An Exhibition of Nanga Fan Painting*; London, 1975.

Irons, Neville John: *Fans of Imperial China*; London, 1982.

Kopplin, Monika: *Kompositionen im Halbrund, Fächerblatter aus Vier Jahrhunderten*;
    Stuttgart, 1983.

Leary, Emmeline: *Fans in Fashion*; Leeds, 1975.

Lipps-Kant, Barbara: *Fächer aus vier Jahrhunderten*; Tubingen, 1983.

Mayor, Susan: *Collecting Fans*; London, 1980.

Niven, T.: *The Fan in Art*; New York, 1911.

Percival, MacIver: *The Fan Book*, London, 1920.

Rhead, George Woolliscroft: *The History of the Fan*; London, 1910.

Salwey, Charlotte M.: *Fans of Japan*; London, 1894.

Schreiber, Lady Charlotte: *Fans and Fan Leaves—English*; London, 1888.

Schreiber, Lady Chgarlotte: *Fans and Fan Leaves—Foreign*; London, 1890.

Uzanne, Octave: *The Fan (English translation by Paul Avril)*; London, 1884.

Walker, Robert: *Catalogue of the Cabinet of Old Fans*; London, 1882.

Acknowledgements

The publisher wishes to thank Christie's Images for kindly supplying all the photography for this book, including the photographs on the front and back covers, with the following exceptions:
Pages 2, 6, 9, 10, 13, 19, 20, 25, 26, 38, 39 (top), 40, 43, 48, 49, 51, 110, 113, 114, 115, 116, 117, 119, 120, 121, 122, 123, 124, 125, 126, 127, 128 and 130-131 courtesy of Hulton Getty Picture Collection;
Page 11 courtesy of © Roger Wood/CORBIS;
Page 15 courtesy of © Pierre Colombel/CORBIS;
Pages 16, 36 and 39 (bottom left) courtesy of © Fulvio Roiter/CORBIS;
Pages 24 and 27 courtesy of Ernst Haas/Hulton Getty Picture Collection;
Page 31 (right) courtesy of © Fukuhara, Inc./CORBIS;
Page 32 courtesy of © Dave Bartruff/CORBIS;
Page 33 (top) courtesy of © Stephanie Maze/CORBIS;
Page 33 (bottom left) courtesy of © Jack Fields/CORBIS;
Pages 33 (bottom right) and 35 courtesy of © Earl and Nazima Kowall/CORBIS;
Page 34 courtesy of © Tim Page/CORBIS;
Page 37 (top) courtesy of © Kevin R Morris/CORBIS;
Page 37 (bottom) courtesy of © Dennis Degnan/CORBIS;
Page 39 (bottom right) courtesy of © Michael S Yamashita/CORBIS;
Pages 52 and 53 courtesy of © Historical Picture Archive/CORBIS;
Page 54 (and detail, right) courtesy of © Leonard de Selva/CORBIS;
Page 55 (and detail, left) courtesy of © Hulton-Deutsch Collection/CORBIS;
Page 132 courtesy of © CORBIS.

Index